MORE THAN WE COULD ASK

MORE THAN WE COULD ASK

*Reaching upward to God
and outward to Others*

Jim Clark

NEW LEAF BOOKS / Orange, CA

MORE THAN WE COULD ASK
published by New Leaf Books

Copyright © 2001 by Jim Clark

ISBN 0-9700836-6-1
Printed in the United States of America

For information:
New Leaf Books, 12542 S. Fairmont, Orange, CA 92869
1-877-634-6004 (toll free)

02 03 04 05 06 07   9 8 7 6 5 4 3 2 1

To

Randy Becton,

whom God used as the spark
to ignite the idea for this book

& Carolyn Dycus,

whose ministry of prayer has been
the kindling to keep this fire going

Table of Contents

Acknowledgements

This book has been a collaborative effort. Many wonderful heroes worked in the background to feed me ideas and pray for its completion. Though I cannot name them all, I do want to especially thank these collaborators:

To the Highland Church prayer ministry team – Your model of passionate prayer helped fuel the writing of many of these chapters.

To Merlin Mann – You have been my editorial advisor, confidante and mostly a prayerful friend.

To Bryan Gibbs – Few people I know have such a steadfast commitment to Jesus and the great commission as you do. I praise God for how Christ lives in you, my brother.

To Lou Seckler – I thank God for our seven-plus years of ministry partnership, and especially for our experiences of going to the throne room together with our struggles, joys and ministry dreams.

To Janie Ramirez – I came to you repeatedly to pray for this book's completion. And you patiently kept on praying.

To our e-mail prayer warriors – What would I do without your work of love as you interceded for this project and innumerable other requests?

To Jane Melton and Carolyn Dycus – As you combed through the final proofs, your eagle eyes helped us dot every "i" and cross every "t".

To Steve and Vanette Hutcheson – Prayer partners deluxe. You believed in this dream and believed in me.

To Tami Weaver – Thanks for teaching me the power of getting on our knees. And not just talking about it, but living it.

To Virginia Vaught – For being a mighty woman of prayer. And for praying that one day I would marry your daughter—years before you even knew me.

To Aaron and Shannon – You bring some of the greatest joys to my life.

To Susan, my bride of 20 years – You are without doubt the greatest source of human encouragement to me. Thank you for allowing Jesus to live in you in such a beautiful way.

To Jesus – Who intercedes for us sinner-saints. May every word of this book bring You glory.

Jim Clark
June 2001

Preface

Randy Becton always has a new dream. This dear brother in Christ and co-worker in the kingdom continually seeks the Lord for fresh and creative new ways for God to use him. He often suggests to me an exciting new vision for my ministry. It was his inspiration and constant encouragement that motivated me to write my first book. Therefore, when he says those magic words, "Jim, I have an idea for your ministry you might pray about," I listen closely.

One Friday early last year, while having lunch together, Randy commented on the growing ministry of prayer at Herald of Truth, the media ministry where both of us work. Having been a partner with me in this ministry for the past seven years, Randy has observed that prayer has become an increasing passion in my life. The Lord continues to lay on my heart a deep burden to bathe every aspect of my ministry in prayer. God has blessed us with a team of volunteers who are always willing to intercede on behalf of people and projects related to this ministry.

At our lunch, Randy challenged me to take this focus to a new level. Pushing his plate away, he said, "Jim, as I was going to sleep one night, I suddenly sat up in bed and felt this strong impression: you need to write a book on prayer." He envisioned a way that the Lord could use me to spread this dream to others. Randy's words grabbed my attention.

Within a few seconds of hearing these words, I somehow knew that Randy was right. The seed was planted. While finishing our iced teas and discussing the potential of such a project, the seed already began to sprout. As I left the restaurant with Randy, I felt that his challenge was a call from God that I could not ignore.

After our lunch I began sketching out ideas for a prayer book. However, this project didn't take off until one Saturday afternoon during the summer. My family was out of town. I had finished all the yard work. It was 100 degrees outside. Escaping the heat, I decided to stay inside for the rest of the day. I nestled into my favorite place to read and think and pray.

I was working through Jim Cymbala's riveting book, *Fresh Wind, Fresh Fire.* As I read of this man's passion for prayer and stories of how God empowered this prayerful church to reach out to the "throwaways" of Brooklyn, New York, God set my heart aflame. That hot summer afternoon, while alone in the cool of our air-conditioned home, I knew that I must write this book.

For the next four hours, while waiting for my family to return, I wrote pages and pages of ideas conceptualizing this book. Stories and concepts came to me so quickly that I could barely write fast enough to keep up. The Spirit of God was energizing my mind with a flood of material to share with those who had a similar hunger and passion to experience God's power through prayer.

As the concept began to develop it became clear that I must have a particular focus. Prayer is such a broad subject and hundreds of good books have been written on the subject. I finally decided on this objective: to provide readers specific ways for their church to develop a prayer ministry focused on reaching lost people. "Prayer evangelism" is a phrase you'll see explained and illustrated throughout the book. I'll define and expand upon this concept in the introduction and throughout the twelve chapters.

This book was born out of several of my experiences in coming to know God's power in my life. For many years the Lord has taught me how vital it is to rely upon Him for everything. He continually calls me to place prayer as the highest priority in my life and ministry.

Throughout the book I offer a number of insights I've received from my research on prayer and how they particularly relate to leading people to Jesus. My own spiritual journey will help illustrate the role of prayer in calling men and women to Christ.

Many dear friends and churches have helped me write this book. You'll read several stories of God's mighty hand at work in response to their intercessions. A number of unsung heroes also helped me write these words. They continually prayed for the Holy Spirit to supervise this project. I thank God for every one of these precious prayer warriors.

My greatest desire is that this book will not only inform and inspire you but will kindle a flame in you and your church to see the living God work more powerfully among your people.

A lost and hurting world desperately needs to know Jesus. Your prayers and your church's prayer ministry could serve to bridge the chasm between a people who are lost and a God who saves. Are you ready to hear the call of God? He has a great adventure awaiting you. A journey you'll never forget, and that will last into eternity.

Introduction

Prayer is releasing the energies of God. For prayer is asking God to do what we cannot do.

Charles Trumbull

Prayer evangelism. Those words may introduce to you a strange new concept. As I look at this phrase I first think that I've combined two different tasks. Prayer is primarily communing with God. Evangelism is proclaiming the crucified and risen Christ to the world. How would we mix these two? I want you to consider for a moment how these two vital aspects of following Jesus can be joined together.

Think of how prayer can serve as a precursor to evangelism. It can be a means of cultivating the ground to make it ready for the gospel seed to be planted. One recent set of events in a South American city beautifully illustrates how these two efforts complement each other.

John Huffman is a missionary in Medellin, Colombia. He has helped pioneer a citywide prayer effort in Medellin that has been extremely effective in bringing people to salvation in Jesus. In describing his strategy, Huffman states: "Our basic idea is to apply the biblical principles of spiritual warfare through prayer before one begins to evangelize."[1]

Huffman's method of spiritual warfare is quite simple. He mobilizes a team to spend two weeks praying for certain neighborhoods prior to an evangelistic campaign. A number of the team members fast and pray for particular groups in the city whom they feel need extra prayer. As his team conducts these prayer vigils, Huffman records the results. The impact of prayer is amazing. During the four years of prayer for neighborhoods in Medellin, the number of evangelical churches swelled from 93 to 140. In addition, the number of believers in Christ escalated by 133 percent.

When a team of evangelists began to distribute literature and enroll people in Bible studies in Medellin, it discovered a significant result of this prayer strategy. In the neighborhoods that had no prayer cover from Huffman's team of prayer warriors, only 10 percent of those they contacted enrolled in the Bible study. In stark contrast, among the people living in areas that had been bathed in prayer, 55 percent signed up to study the Bible. It was clear that God had prepared hearts among those who had received all the prayer.[2]

Huffman's approach is just one means of prayer evangelism. Yet his prayer tactics illustrate the point I'll strive to make throughout this book. I'm firmly convinced that prayer is not just one component of reaching the lost. It is absolutely vital.

In this book I will introduce a variety of approaches to implementing prayer evangelism. You'll learn how churches are revived, ways that God prepares a church for evangelism, and how small groups can become beacons of light for the gospel. You'll read of a shoe shop that was transformed into a prayer room. I'll tell you of some young people with a white-hot passion for reaching their unsaved friends. And I will introduce the concept of prayerwalking, where believers literally walk through neighborhoods and pray for unsaved residents. I hope to encourage your heart as I describe the work of persevering prayer and the story of one family who learned a painful and yet faith-building lesson while remaining steadfast in prayer.

I'll also introduce you to a number of prayer warriors who have inspired me to pray more. God will touch your hearts as you meet...

A passionate woman named Brenda, who felt called by God to pray 2,000 lost souls into the kingdom.

A bold evangelist named Julio, whose courageous leadership spawned a citywide revival that proved very costly to him and his family.

An unassuming elderly man who committed to pray for the ministry of one preacher, leading to a dramatic change in the preacher's ministry and the entire church.

A humble woman named Carolyn, whose steadfast efforts spawned the first organized prayer ministry in her church.

Throughout this book I've woven stories of how the Lord has awakened me in my prayer life (and continues to do so!) and ways He has led me to implement prayer ministries. I've confessed a few of my failures as well as recording a few victories that the Lord has graciously given me. My story is meant to communicate that I'm on this journey with you. I'm asking God to teach all of us new ways to tap into His strength as we prayerfully strive to reach unsaved people.

As the Lord has opened my eyes to the power of prayer, He can do the same for you. He also can awaken slumbering churches that are willing to take prayer evangelism seriously. If just one person who reads the following pages were motivated to begin a prayer evangelism ministry in their church,

I'd consider the hundreds of hours, prayers and research in writing these pages to be worthwhile.

Scripture says, "we are God's fellow workers."[3] The Lord can take weak, sinner-saints, such as you and me, and turn us into mighty warriors of prayer. If you're willing to enter into a new experience of reaching the lost through organized, fervent and passionate prayer, then this book will change your life. Not by my words, but through God's power.

Join me as we take God's hand and allow Him to lead us into the wonder and joy of prayer evangelism.

Notes

1. Peter Wagner, *Churches That Pray* (Ventura, CA: Regal Books, 1993), 182.

2. Ibid., 184.

3. 1 Corinthians 3:9

One

The Awakening

I believe that what the church needs today is not more or better machinery, not new organizations or more novel methods. She needs Christians whom the Holy Spirit can use—Christians of prayer, Christians mighty in prayer.

E. M. Bounds

'Not by might nor by power, but by my Spirit,' says the LORD Almighty.

Zechariah 4:6

Before beginning a prayer evangelism ministry, we need to be convinced in our own hearts that prayer is imperative. Only believers with a passion for prayer are equipped with the conviction and endurance to launch and sustain a ministry of prayer evangelism. God had to break and mold me before I came to the point where these words of Jesus became very real to me: "I am the vine; you are the branches. If a man remains in me and I in him, he will bear much fruit; apart from me you can do nothing."[1]

Thirteen years ago the Lord began to wake me up about how vital prayer was in my relationship with Him. In 1987, my family and I were planning to move to Connecticut and plant a church. Up to that point we had been enjoying a comfortable life and ministry in Memphis, Tennessee. Yet a growing restlessness in my soul created in me a desire to move on and begin something new.

After much thought and discussion, but perhaps not enough prayer, my wife and I made the decision to move to St. Louis. For twenty-one months we would be engaged in training, recruiting and fund-raising to prepare for a church planting. We traded the security of an established church and a steady paycheck for the excitement and instability of giving birth to a congregation. While in St. Louis, we relied on the inconsistent income of donations from friends, family members and a few churches. It was both an exhilarating and frightening experience.

Nine months prior to our move to the Northeast, we still needed to raise a large amount of financial support. The clock was ticking and it was clear we would need some well-established churches and individuals to provide the necessary funds.

One weekend we traveled to Memphis to seek support. I had set up an appointment with Larry McKenzie, the associate minister of a large church. Arriving at the church office early, I anxiously waited for our appointment. I rehearsed my speech. My plan was to ask Larry about the key people most likely to support our domestic mission work. Knowing this church had a strong legacy of funding mission efforts, I sensed that it was an excellent candidate for helping us reach lost people in the Northeast.

Finally, Larry's secretary came out to the reception area and told me that I could go in to see him. After shaking my hand and welcoming me into his office, Larry asked me to sit down. Then came the shocker. Without allowing me to speak a sentence about our mission plans, he launched into a twenty-minute lesson on prayer. This passionate man gave me Scripture after Scripture that urged God's people to pray. He rehearsed

with me the many ways Jesus calls His disciples to depend rad-
ically upon God. He then thanked me for coming and led me
out of his office.

As I left the meeting and drove out of the parking lot, I
thought, "What was that all about? He gave me no chance to
share with him my dreams and goals for mission work." The
meeting felt like a colossal waste of time. This man didn't hear
a word about my objectives or plan of action for church planting. Rather than getting my toe in the door for financial support,
I felt the door slam shut.

It would take many years for me to realize the significance
of that meeting. God didn't give me what I asked, but He certainly offered what I needed. He used Larry McKenzie to teach
me about the high priority for every believer in Christ: daily
dependence upon the living God through prayer. It was a gift
that was far richer than financial support from his church.

Prayer is a Foundation for Everything

Three years after this visit in Memphis, our family moved
to Abilene, Texas. We felt somewhat like a boomerang—being
flung to the Northeast and then eventually circling around and
landing in Texas. Having gone through a difficult experience
in Connecticut, we found ourselves healing in West Texas and
having to re-invent our lives and my ministry. My wife began
to work outside the home. I had returned to school to complete graduate training in Bible and ministry, while working
part time.

During this time of transition, God brought into my life
another man who would take me to the school of prayer. His
name was Michael O'Donnell. He was a man on fire for God.
A professor at Abilene Christian University, he established the
Southwest Center for Fathering. We became kindred spirits the

first time we met. Within a few weeks of our friendship, Michael hired me to assist him in launching and developing this center.

While much of my concern during those wilderness days was to re-establish myself in ministry and become financially stable, Michael's main passion was to know Jesus more and to draw from His Spirit for daily strength and leadership. He knew how to tap into God's power through petitions and intercessory prayer. Without fully realizing it, I was beginning to learn of this power, too. Two moments with Michael were particularly significant in teaching me about prayer.

One moment was when we were working together in his office. Michael turned to me and said, "Jim, prayer is everything." He then launched into an impromptu Bible study on how Jesus calls us to depend continually on Him through prayer. While I realize that there are other vital aspects of leading people to Christ—such as preaching, serving, and studying—as I reflect on Michael's passion for prayer, I see his point. Prayer must be the foundation of all we do in calling people to Jesus.

The other event was on a Friday afternoon when I went to Michael's house. We were preparing to host a seminar that evening and I wanted to review with him some details before the participants arrived. When Michael's wife answered the door, she told me he wasn't available for awhile because he was back in their bedroom praying. While I was wrestling with administrative details, Michael was wrestling in prayer. At first it seemed peculiar for this professor and leader of a growing organization to be hiding out to pray. Yet as I look back on that night, I realize that God was teaching me some vital lessons about the power of humbling ourselves before Him in our prayer closets. It was one more building block of the growing vision of prayer to which God was calling me.

Through Michael's influence, I began to organize prayer vigils prior to each fathering seminar that we hosted. I was hooked. Since those days at the Fathering Center, God has used me to organize prayer vigils for every ministry event in which I've been involved.

As I look back on thirteen years of an increasing emphasis on prayer in my life, I'm becoming more convinced of what Larry and Michael were saying: prayer is the foundation of all we do for the sake of Jesus. It's not just important in evangelism and spiritual growth in the life of the Christian believer. It is essential. I'm discovering that prayer is more than merely obeying a command of the Lord. It is a daily experience of witnessing His promises coming true. Prayer is a wonderful adventure of partnership with the living God.

With Hands Lifted High

One of my favorite stories in the Old Testament is in Exodus 17. The Amalekites were attacking God's covenant people. Moses gave Joshua the most unusual battle strategy, saying: "Choose some of our men and go out to fight the Amalekites. Tomorrow I will stand on top of the hill with the staff of God in my hands."[2]

Moses' outstretched hands were symbolic of prayer. Joshua obeyed his mentor's orders. He fought...and Moses prayed. Notice the connection between prayer and victory over one's enemies: "As long as Moses held up his hands, the Israelites were winning, but whenever he lowered his hands, the Amalekites were winning."[3] Something very significant takes place in the heavenly realm when God's people raise their hearts upward to His throne room. The Lord responded favorably to Moses' pleas. He does the same today.

Partners in Prayer

In our response ministry at Herald of Truth, God has blessed us with many friends who, like Moses, "hold up their hands" on behalf of our work in the kingdom. Seventy friends of the ministry are part of our e-mail prayer team. Approximately fifty other intercessors, who live in our area, are readily available to respond to our requests. Whenever we host an evangelism conference or tape a new series of television programs, we ask our prayer warriors to cover these events with prayer. They join us in calling upon the Lord of life to direct and empower everything we do.

We also regularly send our prayer team the first names of people who have sent prayer requests in response to our television programs and website. These prayer partners join us by interceding for the lost to be reconciled, for believers to grow in Christ and for struggling families and individuals to find the healing and hope they need in the Lord Jesus. One story of answered prayer that I recall is especially touching.

From Despair to Hope

One morning I received a phone call from a distraught woman named Nancy. She had a history of sexual abuse and was under the care of a Christian counselor. When she saw one of our television programs about someone with a similar story to hers, she called our ministry for prayer. Over the past eight years she has been hospitalized for depression ten different times. With her permission, I immediately notified our prayer warriors, urging them to intercede on behalf of Nancy.

Two months later Nancy called back with a very hopeful report on her condition. She told me that a dramatic change had occurred in her life. There was great excitement in her voice as she said:

I'm doing awesome. My mind is clear. I can think now. I'm reading all sorts of helpful books. I have forgiven the people who abused me. All I want to do is read God's word instead of watching TV. God has given me such peace. I have no desire to die now. I want to live!

Nancy is now writing a book on how God has helped her deal properly with her anger and set her free from bitterness. What a wonderful victory our Lord has brought about in Nancy's life. I thank God for how He used the pleas of our prayer warriors as one key element in her healing.

The Power of Organized Prayer

As I witness the Lord continually working in mighty ways in response to our prayers for struggling people such as Nancy, my faith in the power of the living God continues to grow. He is repeatedly confirming to me such promises as: "The earnest prayer of a righteous man has great power and wonderful results."[4]

This week I'm claiming this promise from God's word as I help another desperate person who contacted our ministry. A woman I'll call Hannah read an article I had written on the topic of hope that was posted on a web site. In a four-page e-mail to me, she poured out the bitterness of her soul. Hannah described her disappointments regarding one of her children. Though she could quote some Scripture and said she attended church, it was obvious from the caustic tone of her message that she was angry and disillusioned with God.

After receiving her permission to share her prayer request with others, I asked our team of e-mail prayer warriors to begin interceding for Hannah. Yesterday I sent her a booklet on the gospel and the love of God. I'm confident that the Lord will work on her heart because so many of my fellow believers are lifting their hands to the Father, pleading with Him to work mightily in her life. I'm counting on God to work good out of this very difficult situation in Hannah's life, believing in the power of organized prayer.

As followers of Jesus Christ, you and I are in a battle—a battle for the eternal destiny of men and women. I'm convinced that the Lord will use us in amazing ways as we unite in prayer, asking Him to draw more lost people into His arms of love.

Peter Wagner is an evangelical writer and professor who is also passionate about organized prayer. In his extensive research and visits with growing churches around the world, Wagner has come to this conclusion: "If the intercessors God has placed in each congregation would be recognized, coordinated, trained and released for ministry, churches across America and the world could be completely turned around."[5]

Another researcher on church growth reinforces Wagner's findings. George Barna spoke on the church and the family at a Christian counselors' conference I recently attended. One brief remark he made stood out to me. In his organization's twenty years of research on churches, Barna consistently found that every ministry that involved focused prayer was magnified. He concluded his comments on this finding by saying, "God truly hears the prayer of His people."[6] More importantly, these researchers' discoveries are supporting what our Lord has been telling us all along: "whatever you ask for in prayer, believe that you have received it, and it will be yours."[7]

God Can

Since that unusual meeting in Larry McKenzie's office thirteen years ago, God has repeatedly inspired me to lean on Him for every aspect of my personal life and ministry. It has been a humbling experience, and yet ultimately a positive one. Through His abounding grace, He has done some amazing things in my life in answer to prayer.

Another man has deeply influenced me in striving to depend on God. His name is Bill, a dear friend from my church who is a recovering alcoholic. One of Bill's favorite lines is: "I can't, God can, I think I'll let Him." His wise words echo those of Scripture: "'Not by might nor by power, but by my Spirit,' says the LORD Almighty."[8]

As you walk through the pages of this manual, soaking up practical ideas for prayer evangelism and discovering some of your own, may God grip you with this truth: it is not by our power that we reach lost people with the gospel. Salvation is possible only through the hand of Almighty God.

The good news is that He uses broken, imperfect and willing vessels such as ourselves who will continually pray and witness and serve—allowing Christ to do the drawing...and saving. We can't... God can... Why don't we let Him.

Notes

1. John 15:5
2. Exodus 17:19
3. Exodus 17:11
4. James 5:16, *The Living Bible*, quoted from *The Layman's Parallel Bible* (Grand Rapids, Michigan: Zondervan Bible Publishers, 1973), 2953.
5. Peter Wagner, *Churches That Pray* (Ventura, CA: Regal Books, 1993), 89.
6. George Barna, "Effective Ministry to Today's Families." Keynote speech delivered at the World Conference of the American Association of Christian Counselors: "The Soul of Christian Counseling." Nashville, TN, September 10, 1999.
7. Mark 11:24
8. Zechariah 4:6

TWO

Laying the Foundation

*All true revivals, from Christ's time to ours, have begun
when Christian believers have been struck afresh with God's
incredible holiness—and their contrasting lack of it.*

Evelyn Christenson

While spending time with my extended family in California last summer, I drove by the house where I spent the majority of my childhood. As I slowly circled around the cul-de-sac, memories flooded my mind. I recalled the days when the house was first being built. The contractors spent several weeks grading the lot and pouring the concrete. They carefully set the foundation before building the structure. Forty years later, as I gazed at my old house, I could see that the house was still standing solidly on the lot.

The foundation of a structure is vital. It's true with a building and it's true with a ministry. Before providing you some materials for a prayer ministry, it's vital that I urge you to first lay the foundation. If you and I attempt to implement any ministry that is not established upon this foundation, we'll be standing on the ground of human power rather than on the concrete strength of Almighty God. We'll substitute the flimsy foundation of our ideas and ingenuity for the solid rock of God's will. An incident in Mexico taught me this lesson in a vivid way.

Brought to Our Knees

Five years ago, several couples from our church traveled to Saltillo, Mexico for a four-day evangelistic campaign. Several churches in that city had rented a large ballroom in the hotel where we were staying in downtown Saltillo. Our group had prepared for this campaign for several months. We practiced Spanish songs for our chorus and raised thousands of dollars. Many of our Sunday afternoons were filled with meetings and a crash course in Spanish.

As summer came, we were a finely honed team, ready to take the gospel to the precious people of Mexico. As we drove into Saltillo, with the sun setting behind the beautiful mountains surrounding it, our hopes were high. The next night we gathered early in the hotel lobby for our first evening meeting, eagerly anticipating what God would do.

Suddenly the fire of our enthusiasm was quenched. We noticed a handful of the church leaders rushing toward the front desk. Their faces were somber. Lou Seckler, our speaker for the campaign, met with the leaders and hotel staff. After a few minutes, he returned to our group and called an immediate prayer session, so we hurried upstairs to one of our rooms for the meeting.

Fourteen of us packed into the small hotel room, wondering what had gone wrong. Lou quickly gave us the bad news: a few of the religious leaders in the community had protested our use of a public facility for an evangelistic meeting. They threatened the hotel owners with legal action if our meeting proceeded.

After witnessing God bless the preparation, fund-raising and safe arrival of our team in Mexico, we were shocked at this huge roadblock in our way. Two hours prior to our first meeting, it seemed likely that our campaign would be cancelled.

God had humbled us. He made us realize that only He could clear this major obstacle.

What followed was one of the most touching seasons of prayer that I have experienced. One by one, each team member prayed. Some of us confessed our anger, frustration and confusion. All of us pleaded with the Lord to open this door that had been slammed shut in our faces.

One prayer stood out from the others. Lou, our leader, put his face directly on the floor and cried out to God: "Lord, I am a proud man. You have humbled me today and I needed it." As I listened to his prayer, I was moved by his honest confession. What moved me even more is what happened next.

Thirty minutes after the prayer session, our gracious and powerful God honored our pleas. The hotel management reversed its decision and allowed us to carry on with our meeting for that evening. A large crowd gathered. Lou delivered a potent message. Our chorus sang with joy and passion. And God was glorified.

The Lord gave us a priceless lesson that evening. Before we were to reach out to others with the message of good news, we needed Him to reach into our hearts, bring us to our knees, and burn away the impurities of our pride and self-sufficiency. He reminded us in a painful yet much-needed way that He was in charge. And that He does wondrous things through His people when they walk humbly with their God.[1]

If any ministry, including prayer evangelism, is to be empowered by God, a basic requirement is the spirit of humility, confession and repentance among His people.

The Great Sin

We didn't enjoy being humbled before the Lord during that prayer meeting. It was confusing to all of us. The intervention from outside religious leaders was unexpected. After all our hard work, it seemed unfair for our plans to be disrupted. In retrospect, however, I now recognize that we needed to be humbled. Pride and reliance on our own gifts and efforts creep subtly into our souls. Being brought to our knees was ultimately a deep blessing.

One chapter in C.S. Lewis' *Mere Christianity* comes to mind. It's titled "The Great Sin." Read out loud Lewis' piercing words:

> The essential vice, the utmost evil, is Pride. Unchastity, anger, greed, drunkenness, and all that, are mere fleabites in comparison: it was through Pride that the devil became the devil...As long as you are proud you cannot know God...If anyone would like to acquire humility, I can, I think, tell him the first step. The first step is to realise that one is proud.[2]

A proud person cannot know God. One evening twenty-five years ago, a good friend of Chuck Colson read this chapter to him in his living room. Colson quickly left the house and rushed to his car, trying to disguise his tears. He sat in his car, sobbing with conviction over his sins as he pondered Lewis' words. The Spirit of God penetrated Colson's heart and brought him to his knees. He knew he needed a Savior. A few weeks later he surrendered his heart and soul to Christ.

Since that pivotal evening when he came to terms with his pride, Chuck Colson, a broken and penitent man, has become one of America's premier spokesmen for Christ and a steadfast promoter of prison ministry. But before he was to reach others for Christ, Colson needed Christ to reach him.

I believe the same is true for a church. A proud, self-sufficient body of believers cannot experience the power of Jesus and will be limited in reaching unredeemed people in its community. A proud person cannot know God. A proud church cannot know God well, and thus cannot be a useful tool in His hands.

The Knock on the Door

What is the sign of a proud church? How can I know if my life and my church are being held captive by pride? Here is a litmus test: is your church practicing fervent prayer? Or is it primarily characterized by its incessant activity? When prayer is not the highest priority among a church's leaders, this is a symptom of a self-sufficient body of believers.

The church in Laodicea was notorious for its self-sufficiency. Jesus rebuked this band of believers, saying: "You say, 'I am rich; I have acquired wealth and do not need a thing.' But you do not realize that you are wretched, pitiful, poor, blind and naked."[3] Jesus was left outside of the church, knocking on the door and asking to come in. As Ben Patterson says: "To pray would be to open the door. But our sense of self-sufficiency paralyzes the hand that would turn the knob."[4]

Leading on our Knees

Something significant occurs when believers in Christ get on their knees. My sister-in-law, Tami Weaver, gave me some insights recently about praying on our knees:

> What else do we do on our knees but pray? When you kneel, you're in a position of humility before the Lord. You're admitting your weakness and desperate need for the Lord's power and mercy. And when you kneel, you're more likely to confess your sin and need for a Savior.

Tami has discovered that her greatest times of intimacy with the Lord are when she is on her knees, confessing her sin and communing with her Redeemer. It's her way of "turning the knob" and letting Jesus take more control of her life.

I'm convinced that when leaders in our churches get on their knees together, the Lord exerts His power and blessing in wonderful ways. A recent event in our church beautifully illustrates one way a church can begin "turning the knob."

This past summer, Charles Mattis, one of the shepherds for the Highland Church of Christ, led a Wednesday night meeting on prayer for renewal and revival. He began the meeting by describing signs of renewal in our church. The prayer ministry has steadily grown. A few members restored an old library in our educational wing, transforming it into a prayer room. Prayer vigils now accompany the many summer mission groups that we send out. Charles also recognized the heightened fervor for world missions.

While he rejoiced in all of these signs of revival, Charles reminded the church of how vital it is that we remain humble before the Lord. He then invited all of his fellow shepherds to come to the front and get on their knees. In front of the entire assembly, the elders came forward and in humility dropped to their knees, confessing their sins. Charles concluded the prayer time with an invitation to the rest of the assembly to join their leaders by praying on their knees, if they were physically able to do so.

As these shepherds humbled themselves before the Lord, they experienced what worship leader Joseph Garlington describes as a "grace gate":

> When I am most conscious of my inadequacy, my
> dependence upon God, and upon his sufficiency, that's

when I have "a grace gate"—the inrush of the grace of God for me for a particular reason, a particular season in my life...In my experience, it's the moments I have cried out to God for help, when I felt I least deserved it, that the moment of dependency became for me a grace gate.[5]

Show Me Your Holiness, Lord

Evelyn Christenson has written extensively on prayer and its relationship to evangelism. She tells of when God called her to a time of repentance. On her birthday, she cried out to the Lord, saying, "Lord, show me your holiness and send revival." She then described the Lord's response:

> Immediately, God sent me to Isaiah 6, in which a vision of God's holiness caused Isaiah to cry out, 'Woe is me!' over his own lack of holiness. For two whole weeks, God continued to show me His holiness, while I cried out, 'Woe is me,' to Him. Glimpsing what I'm sure was just a speck of His holiness, I saw the overwhelming nature of my sin.

A while later, God gave Evelyn the opportunity to speak at the National Prayer Committee's first retreat. As she began to prepare her message, the Lord led her to 2 Chronicles 7:14. Although she had read that passage numerous times, during this particular reading the pronouns jumped out at her: "if my people, who are called by my name, will humble themselves and pray and seek my face and turn from their wicked ways, then will I hear from heaven and will forgive their sin and will heal their land."

God was telling her that before revival comes, God's people must stop pointing their fingers at the sins of the world and instead look inward to admit and confess the sins of the church. God sends revival "when we believers confess and repent of our sins!"[6]

While writing this chapter, I'm attempting to put into practice what I'm writing. I'm asking the Lord to renew me and show me His holiness. I must be very honest with you: it's a painful process. He's revealing sin in my life that needs to be rooted out from my heart. As God is giving me a glimpse of His holiness and goodness and power, I'm becoming more in awe of Him. I realize even more how desperately I need His grace and strength. I'm praying that this transformation will result in more effective witness for Jesus.

As the Lord transforms individual believers, He can do the same for churches that become serious about prayer. He'll tear down the walls of self-sufficiency and prepare a church that will be better equipped for evangelistic outreach. A church that bursts with the love and mercy of Jesus cannot help but tell others of His amazing grace.

I'm ready to turn that knob and let Jesus fill me with more of His power. Are you? Come along...let's turn that knob together.

Turning the Knob

How can we allow Jesus to fill our churches with His power and glory? Let me suggest three places for us to begin. First, ask God to burn in your heart a white-hot passion to know Him more. To help you see the majesty, wonder and holiness of Jesus. To cleanse and transform your heart so that you'll feel compelled to tell others about Jesus.

You may question whether your one life could have an impact on an entire church or even on a whole community. When self-doubt rises in your heart, remember this simple statement that a professor shared with me twenty years ago: God plus one is a majority. Consider the impact of just one prayerful man or woman to change the course of history. Moses. David. The Apostle Paul. Augustine. Martin Luther. Mother Teresa. Chuck Colson. You. When Jesus Christ fills the heart of a person abandoned to His will, He'll light a fire that will amaze that believer...and astound those who witness.

Second, find at least one person in your church who has a similar passion for the renewal of the church and for reaching lost souls. Ask him or her to join you in praying for a church-wide revival. God has given me such a friend in Lou Seckler.

Since our early days in Saltillo, Lou and I have become soul mates. For the past seven years, the Lord has knitted our hearts together through weekly prayer sessions. We have prayed hundreds of prayers for our ministries, families and other staff members. Each week we ask the Lord to cleanse and revive our hearts, to renew our church and to empower the Herald of Truth ministry with more boldness in proclaiming the gospel worldwide. God has been faithful in answering those prayers. He has repeatedly showed His mercy to us.

Just today Lou came to my office and rejoiced with me in how he witnessed the Lord work in his recent trip to Guadalajara, Mexico. Many visitors had come to the evening meetings. Lou sensed God giving him the words and passion as he spoke to the participants about God's design for family. One woman came to him afterward and told him a beautiful story of how she was led to Christ. One key element of her conversion was reading a Bible that her daughter had received. Six years ago, our executive director had given this Bible to this woman's daughter at one of our outreach meetings in Guadalajara. Now this woman is our sister in Christ.

You will be amazed to see what the Lord can do in your life and in the life of your church when you begin praying with at least one other fellow believer.

Third, begin praying for the leaders of your church. Ask the Lord to break their hearts, to bring them to their knees. Literally. Pray for God to give them a greater vision of the holiness and majesty of our risen Savior.

A friend of mine is a shepherd in a local church. He described a recent elders' meeting, where one of the shepherds informed them of a major crisis. So serious was the matter, he urged that it would be best for them to pray on their knees. A great sense of reverence filled the room as they all got on the floor to pray. The holiness of God was evident as the overseers of this church literally bowed down before the Holy One. When God brings forth humility among the leaders of His church, revival will follow. He may be calling you at this moment to be an intercessor for your church's leaders, that God's power be unleashed to transform your leaders into more humble, Spirit-led men.

When God Shows Up

Since that small yet powerful prayer meeting in Mexico, the Lord has done wonderful things through our summer mission teams. We returned to Saltillo for two consecutive summers and have seen many people come to Christ. A new church was planted in the city by some of the Christians with whom we ministered. And God changed our lives, too.

Last summer, 41 of us from our congregation, including many of the original team members of our Mexico trips, participated in a life-changing mission campaign to Brazil. All of our children joined us—22 young people who will be forever changed. They're eager to return to Brazil. The Lord has planted in their hearts a passion for missions. The church there has asked us to return in two years for follow-up with those we contacted. They've also invited us to host a Christian camp for high school students. As we continue increasing the prayer focus on these trips, God shows up in wonderful ways.

Before each mission trip, we now plan extensive prayer vigils. We're convinced that Satan will constantly attempt to obstruct our efforts. God has made it clear to us that we need His power to resist Satan and bring people to the Savior. We're "turning the knob" more and seeing Jesus do some amazing work through us.

Renewal from Within

Before a church can effectively reach outward in evangelizing its community, a deep inward renewal is indispensable. Therefore, the foundation for launching a prayer evangelism ministry is a season of individual and corporate repentance, where a body of believers confesses its sins and calls upon the Lord to purify their hearts.

Are you ready for such repentance and revival? Will you join me in turning the knob of that door and allowing Jesus to take more control of our hearts? If so, prepare for God to bring a fresh wave of His power and love to you and your church. You'll never be the same. And neither will your community.

Notes

1. Micah 6:8b

2. C.S. Lewis, *Mere Christianity* (New York: Macmillan, 1943), 94, 99.

3. Revelation 3:17

4. Ben Patterson, "Whatever Happened to Prayer Meeting?," *Leadership*, Fall 1999, 121.

5. Joseph Garlington, "Finding the Grace Gates," *Leadership*, Spring 1999, 26.

6. Evelyn Christenson, "When God Will Not Hear," *Pray!*, Issue 16, January/February, 2000, 16-17.

Three

The God Who Opens Doors

I am not so sure that I believe in the 'power of prayer,' but I do believe in the power of the Lord who answers prayer.

Donald Barnhouse

Don't forget to pray for us, that God will open doors for telling the mystery of Christ.

Colossians 4:3a, *The Message*

It seemed like a chance meeting. In June of 2000, ten families from the Highland Church conducted a nine-day campaign in Itu, Brazil. Our group ended the trip to Brazil with a three-day stay in the beautiful city of Rio de Janeiro. On the last evening we were tired and ready to return to Texas. A few of us walked two blocks from our hotel to a small fast food restaurant.

As we stared at a confusing menu, it was clear we had no idea what we were about to order. At that moment, a young man walked up to us and offered to interpret the menu. His name was Bruno, an attorney who grew up in Rio. He had planned to grab a hamburger before catching the bus for the long ride home. His kindness to us resulted in a very meaningful conversation.

As our family sat down for our burgers and fries, we asked Bruno to join us. For 45 minutes, we had a fascinating discussion with him about God. We told him why we had come to Brazil. Bruno listened intently as we attempted to explain the difference between religion and a personal relationship with Christ. Using a napkin, I wrote down the basics of the gospel—explaining to him that Jesus is the bridge to lead us home to God.

We then gave Bruno the opportunity to share his views about God. He seemed to be a seeker after God, and yet a very confused seeker. Several times he mentioned words such as love and forgiveness, but had great difficulty connecting those concepts with God's word and the truth of Jesus Christ. Near the end of the conversation, he startled us by describing the darkness of the religious practices in Rio. He told stories of the twisted ways that people attempt to communicate with the dead and appease their gods with bizarre rituals.

As the night grew late, we had to end our conversation. After Bruno accompanied us to the hotel, we said goodbye, wondering if we would ever see him again. As we rode the elevator up to our room, I couldn't get this man out of my mind. "This wasn't a chance meeting," I said to myself. "For some reason it seems that the Lord wanted us to talk with Bruno and give him a glimpse of what God longs for His image bearers to experience—a living relationship with a living Lord."

In retrospect, I realized that our encounter with Bruno was the result of our prayers. Months prior to going to Brazil, our team had prayed for God to lead us to lost people. Bruno was one of many persons the Lord put in our path during our time in Brazil.

Opening Hearts

How does God lead the lost to salvation? And in what ways does He use His children in this process? My first response to these questions is that our God is sovereign. He does the draw-ing of people to Himself. Jesus says: "No one can come to me unless the Father who sent me draws him..."[1] We are com-pletely at the mercy of God to draw us to His Son for salvation.

My second response is that even though God is sovereign, amazingly He calls us into partnership with Himself. Almighty God invites us to join Him in these efforts of seeking the lost through our prayers. Notice how the apostle Paul connected prayerful intercessions with reaching lost people: "Devote your-selves to prayer, being watchful and thankful. And pray for us, too, that God may open a door for our message, so that we may proclaim the mystery of Christ, for which I am in chains. Pray that I may proclaim it clearly, as I should."[2]

This mighty evangelist recognized this divine-human part-nership. He urges followers of Christ to offer more than occa-sional prayers. We're to be devoted to prayer. He then asks his Christian friends to plead with the living God to give him occa-sions to share Christ with others. Paul not only asks for God to open doors, but for the Lord to help him clearly communi-cate the good news. In a later epistle, he gives a similar request, saying: "Pray also for me, that whenever I open my mouth, words may be given me so that I will fearlessly make known the mystery of the gospel..."[3]

God is the door opener. The Holy Spirit is the evangelist. His action is clear in Acts 16. Luke describes this evangelistic, Spirit-led moment when Paul spoke to a handful of women at Philippi: "one of those listening was a woman named Lydia... The Lord opened her heart to respond to Paul's message."[4]

I'm convinced that the only way we are going to be effec-tive in sharing Christ is when we unite evangelism with prayer. Note how Jesus invites us to call upon His empowering pres-ence, that we may be His voice and hands in bringing the gospel to others: "Ask the Lord of the harvest...to send out workers into his harvest field."[5]

During my early years as a believer, I failed to recognize this partnership in the gospel that Jesus offered me. In my attempts to bring lost people to our Savior, I relied more on my own efforts than on the Holy Spirit.

Bludgeoned with the Gospel

Nineteen years ago I was enrolled in a two-year Bible school. Part of our training included short-term mission trips. In the spring of 1981, a group of us traveled to New Orleans for a week-long effort to proclaim Christ to the people of this huge city. One of our daily tasks was to walk through neighborhoods knocking doors. Although I dreaded this approach, I joined a partner each morning making "cold calls for Jesus." Our mission was to ask the residents whether they were assured they were going to heaven if they died that night. Unless the person slammed the door in our faces, our next step was to invite them to study the Bible with us.

One incident etched in my mind was an early evening confrontation with some young people. As we were walking down the street, we encountered two teenagers on skateboards who asked us why we came to New Orleans. I quickly launched into a short sermon and confronted them with the gospel. They looked shocked as I bombarded them with Scripture. I gave these boys the right message, but failed to do so with love.

After my surprise attack on these kids, my partner and I walked away. In a few moments he turned to me and said, "Man, you were awfully blunt with those kids." He was right. The sad part of this story is that I never prayed for these two young men. And I certainly didn't pray for God to open a door and help me teach Christ clearly to them. Instead, I bludgeoned these unsuspecting teens with God's word, rather than prayer-fully and lovingly telling them the reason for our visit to New Orleans.

As I reflect further on this campaign, another thing disturbs me—our group spent little time in prayer. If I were to lead such a mission effort again, I would urge us to immerse our evangelistic efforts in prayer. Perhaps we would drive around the city and pray for its inhabitants, rather than condemn it for its notorious immorality. We would start each day with fervent prayer, pleading with the Lord to open doors. An ideal conclusion to each day would involve bringing to the throne room of God the names of people we encountered.

When God Leads

A beautiful contrast to the dismal method of witnessing to those young men in New Orleans is the way my co-worker, Randy Becton, strives to reach unsaved people in our city. He steadily prays for our sovereign Lord to open doors for him to put in a good word for Jesus. As he goes about his day, Randy asks the Lord to help him look through His eyes as he encounters people—the worker at the convenience store who is often overlooked by customers; the lady at the dry cleaners who is having a bad day. When he discovers the names of those he encounters, he adds them to a list and begins asking God to work in their lives. He pleads with the Great Evangelist to lead them to a saving relationship with Christ.

God is sovereign. He draws lost people to Himself through many different means. This work of evangelism is a mystery that you and I can never fully understand. Our part is to trust God to do His work, live in obedience to His word by lifting up Jesus in what we say and do, and continue to pray.

I've repented of my prayerless methods of evangelism,

such as the incident in New Orleans. Today I'm committed to love people to Jesus, be available to tell them about Christ when they're ready to listen and pray for God to transform their hearts. I want to be more keenly aware that God is the One who ultimately opens the doors of people's hearts. My main task is to keep praying for lost individuals I know and be ready to explain to them the hope and joy I have in Jesus.[6]

When Christians Pray for Open Doors

Several months ago I watched a video titled "Transformations." It's a riveting documentary on the fascinating ways that God is opening doors for the gospel in various places around the world. It describes recent accounts of how the Lord dramatically turned around cities that were suffering from the bondage of Satan.

The first story relates the dramatic influence of the Holy Spirit upon Cali, Colombia. At one time Cali was the drug capital of the world. The people in that city, including the police, lived in fear of the drug lords. Fear and crime dominated Cali. Eleven thousand tons of cocaine were exported each year to the United States and Europe. Then God moved in an unusual manner, using a slightly-built church leader named Julio Hoyball.

Julio attended a pastors' meeting and told them how God had given him a burden to pray for their city. He boldly called for Christian leaders to take a stand against the pervasive evil that held the city captive. Julio was convicted that if God's people would set aside their differences and begin an extended prayer vigil, the Lord would hear their cries and create sweeping changes. The other leaders agreed to join him and God began to work in miraculous ways.

In the two days following this initial meeting, there were no murders recorded in Cali. Ten days later one of the drug lords was arrested. Conversions to Christ began to escalate dramatically. The police initiated more arrests of drug czars. Simultaneously, Christians started gathering for praise services in large stadiums.

At one point, through an attack on Julio, it appeared that Satan was successful in stopping this revival. As he continued leading his church and other Christians in the citywide prayer effort, Julio was gunned down by members of the drug world. Although his death appeared to be a great setback for the church in Cali, the Lord used his martyrdom to ignite an even greater revival. In 1995, the mayor declared that the city of Cali, Colombia now belonged to Jesus Christ.[7]

Halfway through the video, a friend watching it with me said, "Now I see clearly what our churches need—to be changed from houses of lectures to houses of prayer." I agree. If the Lord God brought about such an astonishing turnaround to the city of Cali in response to fervent prayer, He can do the same in our communities.

Plowing the Ground

Are we willing to pray such prayers in our churches and cities? As Rick Atchley said, "God can do what man cannot do. With the ministry of the Holy Spirit, He can break through the hardness of men's hearts and grant repentance to people. Before we can sow the seed, we must plow the ground with prayer."[8]

In the previous chapter, I mentioned three ways a church could invite God to empower His people with greater outreach. I now want to suggest three more ways to build upon this prayer focus in order to "plow the ground" with more fervent prayer.

See Through His Eyes

First, ask the Lord to help you begin viewing people through His eyes. Pray that the Lord will give you vision for everyone you meet throughout the day—vision that they are precious creations of God for whom Jesus died. All of us have either heard or made statements such as: "We need to love lost people and reach them with the gospel." Loving people in the abstract is not very strenuous. The challenge arises when we're faced with loving individual persons.

Recently I was in California, attending to my aging parents. One day I went grocery shopping with my Dad at a Trader Joe's store. It was a very "California" store—filled with plenty of earthy people. As we stood in line to buy our food, I was struck by the sight of a young woman behind us. She was in her early 20's and wore all black clothing. The only color on her was her hair. It was bright pink. Dangling from a chain around her neck was a pentagram, a symbol of Satan. The empty look in her eyes repulsed and saddened me. She seemed to be defiant and hardened at such a young age.

I began to ponder the skeletons hidden in the closet of her soul. She may have been abused. She obviously had an emptiness within her. And she was clearly allowing Satan to deceive her. This woman desperately needed to hear that Jesus loves her and would fill her with His peace if she would turn to Him. As we left the store I looked back and hoped to see her also leave. If I spotted this woman again, I thought that I might walk up to her and say I'm praying for her. But I never saw her again. As we drove away I wondered what I would say to this woman filled with such darkness.

I need Jesus to give me the power each day to see people through His eyes and to love them as He loves them. Jesus looked upon crowds and was filled with compassion for them because He knew how desperately they needed Him as their shepherd.[9] This week, attempt to look through Christ's eyes at the checkout person in the grocery store. Rather than rushing through your purchase, take the time to pray for that person. My friend Stanley Shipp is a passionate evangelist. He once told me, "When you ask, 'who is my neighbor?' realize that it's the next person you meet." Every person you and I meet throughout the day is our neighbor. How different our days would be if we began to pray for these neighbors and ask God to work in their hearts.

Focus Prayer Outward

Second, try shifting the focus of your prayers outward. It's tempting to keep our prayers directed to our needs. One way to help us turn outward is to pattern some of our prayers after Colossians 4:2-6. In your Sunday school class or prayer group, begin praying for each other using Paul's requests as a guide:

> To practice watchfulness and thankfulness
> For God to open doors
> For clarity in proclaiming the gospel
> To be wise in dealing with outsiders
> To make the most of every opportunity

During our mission trip to Brazil, God astounded us with the many doors He opened. One morning in the city of Itu especially stands out for me. After breakfast a few of us adults and several of our children walked to a private school, where the teachers had invited us to speak to their students. As we entered the courtyard, we noticed a large gathering of middle school and high school students seated on the steps. It was their morning break and they were awaiting our arrival, eager to hear from these Americans. The school officials set up a public address system and gave us complete freedom to talk for thirty minutes.

Two of the children from our team walked up to the microphone and boldly told the Brazilian students the reason we came to their country—to tell them about Jesus. Another student invited the young people to our evening meetings. Bryan Gibbs, who had been a missionary in Brazil for nine years, delivered a mini-sermon in fluent Portuguese. After our program, many of the students rushed up to our children and began exchanging e-mail addresses with them. I stood in awe of God's work through us. We didn't orchestrate the events of that morning. It was the work of Almighty God. He opened the door and then gave us the privilege of walking through it.

Later that week I sent an e-mail to our home congregation about all that the Lord was doing through us in Brazil. Many members there were part of a prayer vigil on behalf of our mission work. I told them of such incidents as the open door at this school. It was one more piece of evidence that the Lord was responding favorably to their prayers.

What God did for us in Brazil, He can do for you and me each day. Try turning your prayers more outward, asking God to open the doors of opportunity for sharing Christ.

Church-Wide Prayer Vigils

Third, encourage your church to begin an extensive prayer vigil for your community. The creativity and faith of the Richland Hills Church in Fort Worth, Texas continually inspires me. They are a congregation that takes very seriously Jesus' call for His people to pray. Last year they made a bold move. They decided to begin praying by name for a large number of residents living in the area surrounding the church. It was a huge undertaking. Yet they were convinced that God is much bigger than any plan that humans can conceive.

While they prayed, the church began sending postcards to

125,000 homes in North Tarrant County for whom they were praying. The card simply stated that the Richland Hills' Christians were praying for them. A few people called the church and bluntly told them that they could do without prayer. But many more called and expressed their appreciation for the prayer card. And the Lord of the harvest was faithful in answering the prayers of His people. Two hundred and fifty people confessed Christ and were baptized at the Richland Hills congregation during the year of this prayer vigil.

Let's learn from the boldness of this congregation. I believe that God is calling all of us to more boldly and intentionally plead with Him to open doors for us to share our faith with non-believers in our cities.

As I write this chapter, a 40-day prayer vigil is being conducted in our city. Each evening a few prayerful souls gather at a local park to pray. They're asking not only for more physical rain, but also for the "reign of God" to increase in our city. I'm convinced that we will soon witness in our city a fresh harvest of souls coming into the kingdom. When God's people pray, God opens doors.

Constant in Prayer

Each time I walk out of my office, I pass a prayer list posted by the door. On the list are the names of several people we contacted in Brazil. Our team and church are praying for these precious souls—that they will come to know Christ's love and forgiveness. Number five on the list is Bruno—the man we "happened to meet" in a restaurant in Rio. We continue to pray for him to one day be freed from the darkness and confusion that has entangled his soul. We're looking forward to the day he will become our brother in Christ. If Bruno ever sends me an e-mail, I will respond with words of love and encouragement. I'll do all that I can to communicate the gospel clearly to him. And I will continue praying for him, convinced that it is God who unlatches the door of people's hearts.

There are many "Brunos" in our cities. Let's ask God to open more doors and give us clarity of speech and kindness of heart as we share Christ. May we daily surrender our wills to the Lord of the harvest, that we might be more effective tools in His mighty hands. If we do, one day we'll step back in awe as we witness the living God drawing to Himself lost people we know and love.

Notes

1. John 6:44

2. Colossians 4:2-4

3. Ephesians 6:19

4. Acts 16:14

5. Matthew 9:38

6. 1 Peter 3:15

7. Gwen Stein, *Prayer Lines: Official Newsletter of the National Day of Prayer*, Volume 7, Issue 3, Fall 1999, 2.

8. Rick Atchley, "Prayer and Evangelism," Abilene Christian University Lectureship, February 21, 2000.

9. Matthew 9:36

Four

Lighthouses of Prayer

When we are convicted by the idea that those without Jesus are lost eternally, this is when we bombard heaven unceasingly.

Evelyn Christensen

I had the privilege of growing up along the coast of Southern California. One of my favorite pastimes as a teenager was sailing in the ocean with my father. On Saturday mornings when the weather was nice he and I would ride in our 14-foot sailboat out of the local harbor and into the open sea. Some days began with sunny skies and a calm wind. However, the weather would at times abruptly change as the fog rolled in and obscured the sight of the shore. As we attempted to get back to the harbor, our main guide was a flashing light that stood at the tip of the harbor. The light helped us guide our tiny sailboat safely home.

Lighthouses are vital for bringing sailors safely to land. Jesus describes His followers as beacons of His grace: "You are the light of the world...let your light shine before men, that they may see your good deeds and praise your Father in heaven."[1]

I want you to consider how God can work through you and a small group of Christian friends to be a lighthouse for Christ to those near you. In your neighborhood. At the office where you work. Or the school where you teach.

Oswald Chambers reminds us of God's sovereignty in placing us as sources of light among people for whom we can pray:

> God is bringing you into places and among people and into conditions in order that the intercession of the Spirit in you may take a particular line...Your part in intercessory prayer is...to utilize the common-sense circumstances God puts you in and...to bring them before God's throne and give the Spirit in you a chance to intercede for them. In this way God is going to sweep the whole world with His saints.[2]

Two Thousand in 2000

One woman I know recently gave God's Spirit in her a chance to intercede for a particular group of people she wanted to reach for Jesus. In doing so, the Lord began using her as a bright light in the lives of those for whom she prayed.

Brenda Van Dunk teaches at a local university. She's a woman of deep faith in Christ and one who takes very seriously the ministry of prayer. Though I've talked with Brenda many times, one particular day stands out. It was the day we met at a noon gathering in our city on the National Day of Prayer.

I arrived late at the noon gathering, joining a large group of people standing in the shade outside our city hall. After slipping quietly into the edge of the crowd, I glanced at the person next to me and there was my friend, Brenda. After the prayer session concluded, most of the crowd gradually dispersed. Brenda and I lingered for several minutes as she confided in me about a serious health crisis she was facing. She discerned that Satan was attacking her because she and her roommate were involved in a new prayer focus.

One morning earlier this year, Brenda sensed God calling her to begin praying for two thousand souls in the year 2000. In obedience to God's call, she and her roommate initiated a 40 day fast. During that time they asked God to give them specific names of lost souls. They also prayed for others to join them in this prayer vigil.

God has already blessed them with responses to their prayers. Her roommate's brother, who had been away from the Lord for some time, re-commited himself to Christ and is now actively involved in a church. These fervent prayer intercessors are confident in God's power and faithfulness, believing they will witness many more on their prayer list entering into a relationship with Christ.

Lighthouses of Prayer

Brenda and her friend are exemplifying a mission that any group of Christians can easily adopt—establishing a lighthouse of prayer. God unleashes His power in remarkable ways when His children join together to pray by name for people who are away from Christ. If you scan the book of Acts, you will notice that many outbreaks of evangelistic fervor were born in prayer meetings. Prior to Peter's first sermon that led to 3,000 new Christians, the disciples were huddled in an upper room waiting on the Lord. In order to be empowered for this mission, they needed the risen Christ to come among them through the Holy Spirit.[3]

As persecution began to rise in the early church, the Christians assembled and "raised their voices together in prayer to God."[4] They pleaded with the Lord to help them speak boldly about the risen Savior. Heaven came down and gave this small band of believers the zeal and courage to continue witnessing to others about their Lord: "They were all filled with the Holy Spirit and spoke the word of God boldly. With great power the apostles continued to testify to the resurrection of the Lord Jesus, and much grace was upon them all."[5]

In the past two years, a strong current of organized prayer has flowed through our country. It's a movement entitled "Lighthouses of Prayer." Paul Cedar, a key leader in this movement, describes the simplicity of this prayer strategy: "A lighthouse is a gathering of two or more people in Jesus' name for the purpose of praying for, caring for and sharing Christ with their neighbors and others in their sphere of influence."[6]

Lighthouses of prayer take shape in a variety of formats and schedules. Some of the possibilities include:

> A monthly small group on Sunday nights.
> A group of men who periodically meet for breakfast and prayer.
> A schoolteacher or administrator praying for a classroom or an entire campus.
> A receptionist praying for his or her office.
> A department store worker praying for fellow employees.
> A student praying for classmates or teachers.[7]

Prayer, Care and Share

The simplicity of this three-fold approach makes a lighthouse of prayer adaptable to any church or small group of believers who have a heart for reaching lost friends and loved ones with the gospel. You might share this concept with a friend from church or a believing co-worker. Then begin praying together for the Lord to shine Christ's love through you in a brighter way at work or in your neighborhood. Here are some basic ways you might begin:

1. Prayer

Talk to the members of your small group or Sunday class about the lighthouse concept. When God raises up a few of them to establish such an outreach group, allow prayer to be the main agenda of your first meeting. Encourage everyone present to make a list of those they know who need salvation—a neighbor, co-worker, spouse or child. You might suggest that all of you get on your knees and ask the Lord to touch the hearts of each person you've listed. Plead with the Father to equip you with the boldness and love to exert a Christ-like influence on them. As you lift these names before the Father's throne, expect the living God to work on their hearts. Watch for signs that God is moving in their lives.

2. Care

Jesus attracted others to Himself, not only through His words of authority but also through His life of service. He healed, touched, listened and served. Through His Spirit living in us, we can do the same for those within our sphere of influence. Brainstorm with your lighthouse about some creative means of demonstrating God's love towards those for whom you're praying. Ask Jesus to love others through you. Here are some ideas to creatively display Christ's love to neighbors and others with whom you come in contact throughout the week:

> Initiate a block garage sale.
> Be sensitive to senior adults in your neighborhood. Help and serve them around their homes.

Invite your neighbors to your next Christmas party.
Talk to your neighbors about their home, land-
    scaping, and painting.
If you live in an apartment, consider meeting
    neighbors in the laundry room, at the pool or
    exercise room, or at the mailbox.
When someone moves into your neighborhood,
    bake some cookies or a cake and take them
    to the family as a way of welcoming them.[8]

A few weeks ago a friend from church asked me to accompany him on a mission of mercy. He planned to call on several elderly acquaintances that he had met on his "Meals on
Wheels" route. God blessed us with a delightful lunch hour as
we went to several people's homes and told them we were
there simply to pray with them. Nearly all of those we visited
were overjoyed when we arrived on their doorstep. All but one
welcomed us into their homes for a brief time of prayer.

A month after these visits, our education minister sent us an
e-mail reporting her talk with a woman in Dallas. This woman
wanted to thank our church for blessing her mother, one of the
persons we visited on our lunch hour. She said, "When those
men came to my mother's home to pray, she felt as if Jesus had
come to see her."

Praise God for how He used us in this simple act of caring
for some lonely senior citizens. God will astound us in opening
doors to share our faith when we allow Christ's unconditional
love to flow through us.

3. Share

As you pray for specific people in your life, and then serve
them in a variety of ways, expect God to open doors to share

His love with them. I love the story that Al Vander Griend tells of Scott, a minister in Washington, D.C., who caught a vision of establishing a lighthouse of prayer. Scott and his wife asked a couple to join them and begin praying for their neighborhood. They prayed, cared and shared the gospel with those among their circle of contacts. God honored their prayers and concern for others.

One of Scott's neighbors was drawn to this group and eventually led to Christ. The woman asked that her family members and a few friends attend her baptism. Among the friends attending the baptism were the very ones that Scott and his lighthouse companions were asking God to reach. What a thrill it was for this small group of committed prayer warriors to witness God using them to draw men and women from darkness into the light of His love.[9]

Bringing the Gospel to Our Neighbors

Most of the people in our communities will not come to our churches without an invitation. It's likely that only a few would attend if we invited them cold. However, I'm convinced that God will equip us to lead others to Christ if we would begin praying for specific people we know, caring for some of their needs, and sharing Christ when God opens the door.

Let me tell you one more story about Brenda and her "Two thousand in 2000" mission. Since that conversation with Brenda at the National Day of Prayer, a serious development has unfolded in her life. Within a few days after we talked, the doctors confirmed that she had cancer and needed immediate surgery. On the morning of Brenda's surgery, my wife and I had the privilege of praying with her just moments before the gurney arrived to take her to the operating room. Though she was facing a major trial, Brenda was at peace with the Lord.

Later that week our church's congregational care minister visited Brenda in her hospital room. As she walked in the room, her first sight was Brenda's face—aglow with joy and peace. Brenda began to tell her how God had called her to this intercessory prayer ministry for non-believers. Her prayer list had grown to 216 individuals.

Brenda refused to allow Satan to distract her from this mission by sidetracking her with worry over her health. She barely missed a beat during her hospital stay, pressing on with her intercessions for those suffering from the cancer of sin.

The next evening I was scheduled to speak to our church about Epaphras, whom Paul described as one who was "always wrestling in prayer" for others.[10] At the end of my message, a friend of Brenda's stood up and told the story of the year 2000 prayer vigil, her bout with cancer, and her determination to continue praying for the lost.

As we entered into a time of prayer, I asked everyone present to write on an index card the names of friends or family that are away from God. After the class, many people handed me a card. A few of the cards listed more than a dozen names of lost souls. By the end of the week, we sent copies of over two hundred new names to Brenda, who added them to her prayer list.

Brenda is now pleading with the Lord to use her battle with cancer to glorify Him in some way. I believe He's already being glorified. Her story inspired our church to wrestle with more fervency in our prayers for the lost. I'm also convinced that as you read her story, God will touch your heart and prompt you to seriously consider starting a lighthouse of prayer to reach lost people you know. Brenda would be thrilled to hear how God used her prayer ministry and health crisis to inspire others to become beacons for Jesus.

Before you put down this book, would you consider initiating a lighthouse movement in your church? It could start as simply as asking one friend from church to join you in implementing some of the ideas from this chapter. Just try it for a few weeks, believing that the Lord will work as you pray, care and share.

You could be another "Brenda" to ignite a flame of fervent prayer for those far away from the light of Christ. May His light beam brightly from your own lighthouse of prayer and may He give you the joyous opportunity of welcoming men and women into the safe harbor of God's love.

Notes

1. Matthew 5:14a, 16b

2. Oswald Chambers, *My Utmost for His Highest* (New York: Dodd, Mead and Company, 1935), 312.

3. Acts 2:1-41

4. Acts 4:24a

5. Acts 4:31b, 33

6. Paul A. Cedar, "The Lighthouse Movement," *Pray!*, Issue 15, November/December, 1999, 18.

7. *Neighborhood Lighthouses of Prayer—Information Manual, Pray Big Country* (No author given), 1.

8. Ibid., 9.

9. Al Vander Griend, "A Marriage Made in Heaven," *Pray!*, Issue 15, November/December, 1999, 22.

10. Colossians 4:12

Five

Establishing a Prayer Room

*Allow yourself and your church to take prayer as seriously as
you take education, worship, outreach, and fellowship.*

Al Vander Griend

Who would have thought that one room in a church
could be so important? It took many years for me to
make this discovery. Now I'm convinced that such a room is
vital to churches that place prayer as a high priority.

I've been thinking lately of the many churches I've been
connected with in the past 23 years. For eleven years I was a
vagabond, living in nearly every part of the United States. God
has used these numerous relocations to give me a wide array
of ministry experiences with several churches—in California,
Texas, Arkansas, Tennessee, Missouri and Connecticut.

With the exception of the church in Connecticut (a new
church planting that met in a rented office complex), each
one of these congregations had an auditorium, classrooms,
bathrooms, a nursery, a kitchen and a fellowship hall. Every
one of these spaces served important functions for the body
of Christ to worship, learn, and enjoy Christian fellowship.
However, there was one room these churches lacked—a
room dedicated to prayer.

At the time, this missing element of a church didn't bother me, since I had never thought of such a room. Quite honestly, for my first seven years of full-time work with churches, prayer was not my greatest concern. My primary focal points were studying for classes, pastoral counseling, and organizing fellowship and service activities. I was an activist, a visionary minister who wasted too many years allowing prayer to fall to the bottom of my "To Do" list—or not even finding a place on the list.

During those years of much activity and little prayer, God was patient with me. He continued to knock on the door of my heart, inviting me to rest in Him and rely upon Him for everything. In some unusual ways He revealed to me the value of retreating to particular places for prayer. One setting quite vivid in my memory is a beautiful room overlooking an ocean bay in Connecticut.

A Retreat for the Soul

Twelve years ago, when my family was involved in planting a church in the Northeast, God gave me a wonderful partner in ministry, Dan Creech. While I leaned toward an action style of leadership, Dan practiced a more contemplative, prayerful style. We were both a great balance and an occasional source of frustration to each other.

One of the greatest gifts Dan gave me was an invitation to join him on a weekly pilgrimage to a retreat site. Each Friday morning, he and I traveled forty minutes to the Mercy Center, a gorgeous renovated estate along the shores of Eastern Connecticut. Some very gracious Catholic nuns operated it. I can still feel that sense of calmness invade my soul as I recall walking in the courtyard of this peaceful place.

On my first visit to the Mercy Center, Dan introduced me to the Sisters of Mercy, who kindly welcomed us at the front desk. He then escorted me to a large living room furnished with an assortment of comfortable chairs and couches. The room was strategically built overlooking the ocean. His words startled me when he announced, "I'll see you in three hours." Inside my soul I screamed, "Three hours? How am I going to pray all morning? I need this time to work on my sermon for Sunday." Swirling through my mind were the many tasks before me. I had several phone calls to return and outreach programs to implement. My supporting churches were waiting for reports about all the people we were reaching. I wondered how I could justify looking out at the ocean for three hours and "just praying." My flesh was crying out to stay in control, while God's still small voice was quietly wooing me to lie still beside His quiet waters.

Later that morning, after meditating on the book of Ephesians and praying for the longest time I had ever prayed, it became clear that this morning of prayerful reflection was an extremely valuable use of my time. As those weekly retreats continued, I began to surrender to the Lord my drivenness and desire to be in control. Those Friday morning meetings with the Lord became precious moments that I craved. The living room, with its soul-calming ocean view, became a treasured sanctuary to me. Dan was right—I needed a weekly refill from the Lord. I desperately need to emulate Jesus, who regularly sought time alone with His Father. He was teaching me to be still and know that He is God, and I'm not.

From Soles to Souls

It would take eight years after that experience for me to grasp the vision that churches can create places like that setting in Connecticut. Though their building may be hundreds of miles from a mountain cabin or a house on the beach, churches can still set apart such "sacred spaces." One church in our city did that recently, but in a very unusual way.

A Methodist church with a passion for intercessory prayer caught a dream for transforming a building next to their youth center into a place for significant ministry. The building was the site of a shoe repair shop that closed its business. The members of this church purchased the property, poured $50,000 into its renovation and created a beautiful prayer room. One person told me that the building has changed from a shop to repair soles to a haven for the healing and saving of souls.

I got to know the minister at this church, Tom Thompson. One day I asked Tom if I could visit the prayer room and he graciously gave me the code number of the outer door, offering me the use of it any time I please.

What a rich gift the use of this prayer room has been to me. Though it doesn't have an ocean view, this room has been a place where I've enjoyed many sweet moments with the Lord. A few times a month I'll slip into the room for some solitude and communion with the Father. Prior to teaching a class or in the midst of a writing project, I may take my notes to this sanctuary of silence and pray over them. Several months ago I took the outline and files for this book to the prayer room and offered it all to the Lord. Occasionally my wife and I will go to the room together, getting on our knees and praying for our marriage, our children and others we love. God has always blessed everything I've prayed about in this prayer room.

One early Sunday morning was especially meaningful. At five in the morning, I woke up with a heavy heart, worrying about a situation with one of our children. Unable to sleep, I crawled out of bed, quietly left the house and drove to the prayer room. For several minutes I knelt at the bench, pleading with the Lord to take care of this problem. Eventually I sat down on one of the wingback chairs, stopped my travailing in prayer and remained still for a few moments. I recall so well hearing these words in my soul: "Surrender, Jim, surrender. Give your children to me. I'll take care of their lives and their souls." For several minutes I sat in the stillness of that room, turning this worrisome situation over to Jesus. The serenity of that moment made it difficult to leave. God had given me peace about a burden that had been so weighty two hours earlier.

An Outward Focus

After several visits to this prayer room, I noticed that it had a particular focus—praying lost souls into the kingdom.

Mounted on one side of the room is a map of our city. Flanking the adjacent side is a padded kneeling bench. Several prayer requests are placed along the shelf above the kneeling area. For a number of weeks I noticed a photo of a teenage girl with a note attached to it stating: "Please pray for this girl to be delivered from Satan's grip." A few months later someone placed another note to the photo, giving thanks to the Lord that this girl had turned her life over to Jesus.

I will often glance at the monthly calendar, praying for the names of unsaved friends and family listed on each day of the month. This is a room that draws visitors into the ministry of prayer evangelism.

Birth of a Prayer Room

Four years ago, a handful of Christians from the Highland Church sensed God calling them to more intentional prayer. A local prayer seminar ignited in their hearts a desire to implement an organized prayer ministry at Highland. One of their first agenda items was establishing a prayer room. They began to dream about and ask God for a fitting site in our building that could be designated for prayer.

After much prayer and searching for a room, they witnessed the Lord open the door for this dream. An upstairs room of our education wing was vacated by a church staff member and offered to the prayer ministry. They quickly dedicated the room as a central place of intercession. Terry Browder, a long-time member of Highland, offered to help decorate it. Using his excellent tastes and decorating gifts, Terry furnished the room with his own antique furniture and oriental rugs. He replaced the fluorescent lights with a lamp equipped with a dimmer to create soft lighting.

Volunteers painted the walls in a soothing burgundy color. One person donated a phone and answering machine that is now being used to record a 24-hour flow of prayer requests. Adorning one wall is a cloth-bound board with a variety of crosses attached to it. Since its inauguration, this prayer room has become another "Mercy Center" to me. My heart is full of memories of significant prayer moments: several of us surrounding a high school student with a brain tumor; being prayed over by some friends while I was suffering a bout of depression; and being on my knees, wrestling in prayer, minutes before teaching an auditorium class on ways to pray for lost people.

With the completion of a new education building at our church, the prayer ministry is now blessed with a new prayer room with outside access. Our leaders have caught a vision for prayer. By designating one room for prayer in our new building, they're making this significant statement: God's people are to be about the ministry of intercession.

I'm very aware that a Christian or group of believers can talk to the Lord at any time or in any place. We don't need a Mercy Center to commune with God. The Holy Spirit does not dwell in a building made by human hands but in the temple of every believer in Christ. Through Jesus Christ we have the distinct privilege of communing with the Father at any time of day, at any place in the world. But I am also deeply convinced that designating one room for intercessory prayer can exert a profound impact on a church and community. Could your church dedicate one room for prayer, a room where the focus would be on interceding for unsaved people? Perhaps God is calling you to be a catalyst to create such a room.

Initiating a Prayer Room

If you and at least one other person at your church are sensing a burden from the Lord to establish such a room, start meeting together and seek the Lord's will and timing for such a room. Here are a few suggestions on how to create and develop a prayer room.

First, walk through your church building before or after worship or class times. Quietly ask God to lead you to a room that would be an ideal setting for praying for the community, your leaders and struggling believers. Begin meeting once a month with others interested in a prayer room and an intercessory prayer ministry. Share your ideas with one another and stay united and fervent in going to God's throne room until you see Him move mountains in your church. Claim the Lord's promises from such verses as Ephesians 3:20: He "is able to do immeasurably more than all we ask or imagine, according to his power that is at work within us."

Second, pray for the Holy Spirit's guidance. As Psalm 127:1 tells us, "Unless the LORD builds the house, its builders labor in vain." Allow the Great Architect to build this prayer ministry, in His way and on His timing. Realize that others in your congregation might not be ready for such a room or haven't yet caught a vision for this kind of prayer ministry. Let's be very honest—church politics will likely throw roadblocks in your way when you begin asking for a room dedicated solely for prayer. Prepare for some resistance. Everyone values "their" office, classroom or workroom. Before you begin asking your leaders for a room, go to the Lord first and plead with Him to go before you. When you allow God to direct you in the right timing and space for such a room, you'll be less likely to force this dream on the rest of the church.

Third, seek out a room of suitable size and location. Ideally, the space should be easily accessible to your members and have an outside entrance. While easy access is important, it's also recommended that the room not be too close to a room where large groups gather. Such a place may seem impossible to locate, but remember that our God is able.

Fourth, furnish the room with an evangelistic thrust in mind. While you certainly want to provide resources for praying for the sick and other temporal concerns, be sure to equip the room with tools that emphasize intercession for lost or straying souls. Mount on one wall a framed map of your city. Consider installing a kneeling bench. Place in front of the bench a slightly tilted, waist level shelf so that those who kneel can read their Bible and look over the various prayer requests on the shelf. Whenever people turn in requests for prayer, especially for prodigals and those in rebellion to God, place those cards on the shelf.

Ask some members with talent for decorating to help create a warm, inviting atmosphere for those who come to pray. As you continue seeking the Spirit's leadership and provision, expect some members of your church to donate furnishings and money to equip the room.[1]

The War Room

Early last summer, my niece and her husband were blessed to visit London and Scotland. One of their favorite tourist spots was an underground bunker in London. They were fascinated with the famous war room where Winston Churchill met with his military leaders to plot Germany's defeat in World War II. Major turning points of the war and the history of Western Civilization occurred through many of the strategies developed in that war room.

We have been commissioned by the King of Kings to go to battle for people's souls. Our weapons are the gospel of peace and the instruments of prayer. Establishing a "war room" in our church buildings provides a designated space for doing battle with the enemy. I have seen the Lord bring about some major turning points in people's lives through the fervent prayers offered to God in a prayer room.

I thank God for the revival of prayer occurring among His people today. One of the signs of this revival is that churches are recognizing that having a prayer room is just as vital to the life of Christ's body as a worship center and classrooms.

May the Lord move in your heart to help create such a room. As the former shoe shop has been for me, this room may become your favorite place in the church building. It will likely be a setting where hundreds of prayers will rise up to God's throne on behalf of lost people. In response to your prayers, God will change history...including your own.

Note

1. These ideas were derived from the notes of the Highland Church prayer ministry. For further suggestions on setting up a prayer room in your church, see Appendix A.

Six

Lighting the Torch

*Corporate prayer was not peripheral back when the Church
was established after the day of Pentecost. It was central.*

Peter Wagner

Recently I was privileged to attend a "Prevailing Church Conference" at the Fellowship Church in Dallas. In the past 10 years, this church has exploded in growth, mushrooming from 150 to over 9,000. Though I was there for only 24 hours, I could feel the throbbing pulse of this church, whose lifeblood is bringing seekers to the cross and fresh new life in Jesus.

One keynote address was given by Bill Hybels, founder of the largest church in America, the Willow Creek Community Church. He delivered a riveting message on vision casting. One statement in particular stood out: "Legislation will never transform a human heart. Nor will business. Nor will the internet. Not even education. Our world changes one person at a time. Only one power can change a person—the power of Jesus Christ. And He uses the local church."

Bill concluded his talk with this challenge: "Your church really does represent the hope for the world. There are many people in your communities who need Christ. Will you and I pay the price and take the risk to reach these lost people for Jesus Christ? When you see people come into the kingdom as freshly redeemed children of God, you'll realize it's all worth it." He then showed us a beautiful video of a baptismal service at a pond outside their building. God gripped my heart as I watched several new converts to Christ being buried with the Lord and rising up in joy.

Before leading us in prayer, Bill challenged us with these words: "we have no idea how many days God has given us. I plan to use my remaining days to reach lost people through the local church." As I heard Bill express the deep passion of his heart, I prayed silently, "Lord, with the remaining days You give me, I, too, want to lead many people to You."

The following Monday, I joined some of my co-workers to process the seminar. The burning question in our hearts was not just, "How could we use the training and inspiration from this conference to augment our ministries in the U.S. and Mexico?" We also asked each other, "What does this mean for our relationship with lost people?"

I could have allowed the impact of the conference to send me into a downward spiral of guilt and frustration. In your honest moments you may admit that you share some of these feelings. I'm proposing that instead of remaining immersed in guilt we become more intentional about praying for more fervent evangelism. We can use this sense of inadequacy to drive us to the Lord and say, "Father, please replace our weakness with Your power so we can bring more people to the cross."

An Assembly of Power

When I envision God's people being united in prayer, the story of Acts 4 surfaces in my mind. The religious leaders were livid with the apostles for healing the lame man and preaching the risen Christ. They called Peter and John before the Sanhedrin and attempted to quench the flames of their zeal. Yet it was impossible for these disciples of the Lord to contain the good news burning in their hearts.

After their release, Peter and John returned to their brothers and sisters to report God's victory. A spontaneous prayer and praise time erupted. "They raised their voices together," and God visited them in a mighty way.[1]

God does some amazing things when His children raise their voices together in prayer...

> He shakes the meeting place. (vs. 31a)
> He fills His people with His power. (vs. 31b)
> He gives them boldness to proclaim the word of God.
>   (vs. 31c and 33)
> He creates sweet unity among the saints. (v. 32)

I'm wondering...what would the risen Lord do among us as believers today if we would gather together and ask God for more boldness in telling others this great news? God's word convinces me that the same Jesus who worked among the first-century church works among Christians today who recognize their weakness and are open to experiencing the power of almighty God.

Praying for Prodigals

In November of 1998, the movie, "The Prince of Egypt," was about to be released. To prepare us for seeing this excellent animated film, our preacher, Mike Cope, delivered a series of lessons on the book of Exodus. One Sunday in particular was especially moving.

As I entered the auditorium with my family that morning, I noticed a distinctive change in the front area. On both sides of the pulpit stood two large tables. Placed on each table were stacks of blank white cards, pens and a basket. I knew that we were about to experience an unusual morning of worship.

Mike described the scene in Exodus 14, where the Lord displayed His awesome, saving power by parting the Red Sea. He then stressed that our God is still in the delivering business. In a few moments, we all realized the purpose of the tables. Mike asked us to think of loved ones—children, grandchildren, extended family members, and friends—who were away from the Lord. He called us to come to the front and write on the cards the first names of prodigals who needed prayer for God's deliverance.

The reaction of the congregation was astounding. By the time I reached the front, I had to wait in line to write down my names. There were too many people gathered around the tables. One elder later told me that it looked as if people were shot out of a gun as they rushed to the tables to write down names of loved ones.

To conclude this time of intercession, one member gathered the two baskets, overflowing with cards, literally lifted them before God, and prayed. We all joined him in pleading with the Lord to bring these prodigals home. After the service, our prayer ministry took the stack of cards to our prayer room. They counted 1,019 names of lost or straying loved ones. In the next few weeks, the prayer team brought these names before the Father's throne. Although we realize only the Lord knows how He is working in these people's lives, we have received some glimpses of His mighty work. One friend told me that his daughter's name was on one of those cards, and that she came to Christ a few months later.

That special worship time spoke loudly to us about what burdens the hearts of believers. The swarms of people around those tables revealed a church that aches over family members who have strayed from the body of Christ or have never come under the protective covering of Christ's blood. This event also revealed the truth that when the saints are asked to pray for the lost (especially those close to them), they will respond enthusiastically.

Silent Prayer Servants

A second event at our church confirmed to me the wondrous things our Lord can do when the body of Christ unites in prayer. At Easter time, Mike began a two-part series, centered on the cross and resurrection. On the Sunday before Easter, he emphasized the death of Christ; on Easter morning his sermon focused on the resurrection of our Lord. At the end of each lesson he challenged people to give their lives to Christ that week or on Easter Sunday.

At both services two of our elders announced that several new births had taken place that week. As Mike concluded his sermon in the second service, he announced that he was going back to the baptistery to change clothes and await those who are ready to accept Christ. Two people came forward, with a repentant heart and a desire to receive the grace of God. All of us witnessing God at work couldn't help but break out in applause as we saw these two young men rise out of the water as new creations.

Why such a tremendous response to the gospel that particular week? Very few of our members were aware of what had occurred behind-the-scenes. Throughout the week, Highland's prayer ministry collected e-mails from members sending in names of people needing salvation. On Saturday night before Easter, our prayer team met at the auditorium to pray over the podium and all the pews. They firmly believed in

God's promises that when His people pray, He acts. As I witnessed the number of responses to Christ that Easter morning, I envisioned that small, yet potent cluster of faith-filled believers on their knees in our auditorium the night before. God had honored their faith and prayers.

There are numerous ways a church can come before the Father's throne, either as an entire body or in small clusters of prayer warriors. Let me suggest a few ideas that provide some places to begin.

Praying Over Leaders

First, if you sense God calling you to this aspect of a prayer ministry, begin asking Him to lead you to others at your church with a similar passion for focused and organized intercession. I recommend that you start small.

John Maxwell tells of a time when God awakened him to the power of having others pray for him. Having been at a new church in San Diego for only six weeks, John was busy getting to know the church leaders and planning a strategy for the congregation. In his study one morning he noticed an appointment with a man named Bill Klassen. When he asked his secretary who this man was, she informed him he was not a leader and that, in fact, he wasn't even a member of the Skyline church. Being task-oriented, John told her, "Give me about fifteen minutes with him, and if we're not done, interrupt us." John's plan was to quickly figure out this man's agenda, try to fix his problem and then get on with the important work for that day. He had no idea that God had specially arranged this appointment.

Bill was a wise, silver-haired man who quietly declared that God had called him to pray for Christian leaders—including John. Suddenly, Maxwell's driven schedule screeched to a halt. He had never had a person come to him with the sole agenda of praying for him. He was most often the one who was to do the praying. That day initiated a radical transformation of Maxwell's ministry.

The next Sunday Bill and his wife were seated in the front row, praying for John as he preached God's word. Bill went on to become Maxwell's personal prayer partner and organizer of a prayer partner ministry for the entire Skyline church. This group of 120 prayerful supporters continually prayed for John. Over the next fourteen years, the church tripled in size, swelling to 3,500 members. The church's annual income jumped to more than $5,000,000. Thousands of people came to Christ. Maxwell eventually became a primary spokesman on Christian leadership. Reflecting on that pivotal moment in his life, he says: "Without prayer and the power of the Holy Spirit, I believe none of these things would have happened. The glory and the honor belong to God. But the credit for releasing that power and keeping me protected day after day belongs to those prayer partners."[2]

A few weeks after reading this book, I felt prompted by God to go to our preacher and pray for him. A fellow member at Highland accompanied me as I went to Mike Cope's office. Initially, he was oblivious as to why we came to visit him. Perhaps he thought we'd come to share a grievance about his preaching. The expression on Mike's face turned to relief when he realized that our sole intention was to pray for him. Knowing that Mike was about to embark on a new series on Romans, we asked him if we could lay hands on him and pray God's special blessing upon him and these messages. We were convinced that before Mike was to give, he needed to receive.

You might do the same for your ministry staff. Consider asking interested members of your church to commit to pray for your preacher for a three to six-month period. If you are part of a multi-staff church, assign a prayer partner to each minister. Set up appointments with the staff members and the one willing to pray for them. Then watch God work as He empowers and transforms the ministers and those to whom they minister.

Prayer-Empowered Worship

Second, as a team of prayer warriors forms, begin scheduling them to intercede during the worship hour. Find individuals willing to spend at least one hour, perhaps once a month, pleading with God to work His will in those who proclaim God's word, in others leading worship and in the hearts of the worshipers.

While on a weekend retreat three years ago, I was asked to pray one Sunday in a makeshift prayer room. My task was to ask Almighty God to empower the man preaching that morning. At first I was very concerned that I would run out of things to say during my prayer time. In a few minutes, however, I sensed God providing me a very simple and yet effective structure for the prayer—praying His word. I opened to the book of Ephesians and slowly began to pray the word of God—not just read it, but pray those inspired words of Scripture. I asked the Lord to infuse this man with strength to say things that were beyond his human strength. I pleaded with God to open the hearts of the listeners, as they heard the message of the gospel, that "the eyes of their heart would be enlightened" so that they would know Christ better.[3] Although I spent a long time in that prayer room, I didn't run out of words or ideas for prayer.

In two weeks I'm scheduled to pray in our church's prayer room during the first assembly. There's little worry in my heart as to how I'll pray. God's word will be my guide. The Lord will give me the words as I pray during this assembly—for the lost to be found and the saved to be strengthened in Christ.[4]

Appointed Days for Congregational Prayer

Third, choose a day or two during the year where your church will focus upon praying for lost friends and family members. Ask the Lord for ideas on how your church could dedicate certain days for intercessory prayer. These suggestions could give you a start:

> During weekly worship times, periodically dedicate one prayer to asking God for more boldness in proclaiming Jesus to lost friends.
>
> Designate one Sunday night every few months as a prayer night for lost souls and straying Christians.
>
> Once a quarter use some of the Sunday morning class time to pray for acquaintances and family who are far from Christ.

James 4:2 says, "You do not have, because you do not ask God." As you begin dreaming about and implementing these prayer events at your church, envision God doing some unprecedented things among you. Perhaps a year from now, people from other churches and communities will be asking, "What is going on at that church? Why is it growing so rapidly? What is the key to their evangelistic fervor?" You can humbly respond, "By God's grace, we have because we asked Him."

Lighting the Torch

On that Friday evening when Bill Hybels spoke to us about his passion for reaching lost people, he gave us a fitting imagery of a church on fire for Jesus. Near the end of his message, he picked up his red Bible, curled it up and said, "Imagine this as a torch. Lately, our church has been asking God to light a torch underneath us and ignite an even greater fervor for evangelism." He then described a three-week Wednesday night series in their New Community class. John Ortberg, the church's teaching pastor, provided the believers with evangelism training on how to become contagious Christians. On each of the three Wednesday nights his class broke up into small groups and scattered throughout the auditorium. These clusters of caring, passionate Christians prayed fervently by name for lost people within their web of influence. The torch was lit, and the flame of outreach was sure to follow.

As I'm writing this chapter, a large portion of the landscape of Montana is being incinerated by brush fires. Our president visited this beautiful state last week, declaring the torched land a disaster area and promising millions of federal dollars for reconstruction.

I'm wondering how that fire began. Perhaps it was arson. Or a careless camper. I'm not sure of the specifics and yet I'm speculating that this massive, raging fire began very small. It may have been started by a single match.

You may be a match in the hands of God. He is ready to strike your heart on the matchbook of His Holy Spirit. The Lord could use you to begin burning with a white-hot zeal for Jesus, sparking a revival sweeping through your entire church. God can take that spark in your heart, even if it's a tiny flickering flame, and equip you to call others together for more united and bold prayers for the lost.

Get ready for the building to shake. And the flames to spread. And prepare to witness the lost in your community being drawn to the warmth of God's love.

Notes

1. Acts 4:24

2. John Maxwell, *Partners in Prayer* (Nashville: Thomas Nelson, 1996), 1-4.

3. Ephesians 1:18

4. See Appendix B, "Praying During the Worship Hour," for a more complete list of how to pray for worship leaders and worshippers during Sunday morning assemblies.

Seven

Persevering Prayer

The great point is never to give up until the answer comes. I have been praying for 63 years and 8 months for one man's conversion. He is not saved yet, but he will be. How can it be otherwise? I am praying.

George Muller

Is there one person in your life whom you love dearly and yet has not yet confessed the name of Christ? Have you been praying for many years, perhaps decades, for him or her to come to know the love of the Father?

Now for the challenging question: have you felt at times that the loved one for whom you're praying may never turn his or her heart to God? So have I. Perhaps the most difficult task of a follower of Christ is persevering in prayer. Not giving up. Continuing to believe that some how, some way and some day God will answer our prayers.

Help My Unbelief

A man with the alias of William Hanford opened up his heart as he candidly described a parenting ordeal. His adult son had joined a cult in a state far away from home. William and his wife, Carolyn, were crushed and felt absolutely helpless.

Some well-meaning friends urged them to immediately fly out to see Kevin and force him to come home. Acknowledging that he was an adult, Kevin's parents chose another route.

As they sought God's guidance, they sensed Him calling them to an intense period of prayer for their captive son. Each day—in their cars, at work, together in the evenings—William and Carolyn pleaded with the Lord to deliver their son from the darkness of the cult. Night after night, before going to sleep, they committed him into the hands of God.

One evening, while searching for Scriptures to soothe their aching souls, they came across a familiar passage. It was a story of another parent in despair. Mark 9 describes a father whose son was afflicted with a demon for many years. He brought the boy to Jesus. The Lord assured him that all things were possible to those who believe. The hurting father replied with words that we might say in our honest, desperate moments: "I do believe; help me overcome my unbelief!"[1] Perhaps that's all the faith this weary father needed as he laid at Jesus' feet this "hopeless case" of a demon-possessed son. The Lord rebuked the evil spirit and healed the boy. He later explained to His disciples, who were perplexed over why they couldn't heal the boy, "This kind can come out only by prayer."[2] Some of life's challenges become so overwhelming that our only recourse is prayer—as Kevin's Dad came to believe.

While William was reading this familiar passage, God gave him the hope he had sought so earnestly. He simply needed to keep trusting God for his son's return. As he read the passage to Carolyn, she quickly grabbed the Bible and read it out loud. With tears in her eyes she replied, "Write in the margin of that passage, 'We believe.'" He quickly wrote the date, Kevin's name and the words, "We believe." For the next several days they continued to pray, wait and hope...and believe.

One evening after dinner, William hopped into his car to run some errands. As he pulled out of the driveway, his wife came running outside with her arms waving. She yelled, "Kevin is on the phone and he wants to talk to you." This hopeful father rushed in the house, picked up the phone and heard these precious words from his son, "Dad, can I come home?"

Within an hour William had booked a flight for his son's return. Kevin flew through the entire night. The next morning this family was blessed with a sweet reunion at the airport. The prodigal son fell into the arms of some very thankful parents. It was one month to the day that William had written in his Bible those simple, faith-filled words: "We believe."[3]

Praying for Prodigals

While it thrills us to hear of such family reunions, these stories may leave some of us a bit envious. We long for our own prodigals to come home. We know what's best for them—to experience the joy of the Lord and the peace of Christ. I became acutely aware of this thorn in the side of believers when I interviewed several parents in pain.

After hearing many stories of heart-broken friends from around the country whose adult children were away from God, Randy Becton and I felt God calling us to produce a resource to help these hurting parents. The result was the "Homecoming" kit. This resource is a set of videos, audiotapes and booklets that minister to parents with prodigals. Also included in the set are messages of God's love to those who have drifted from fellowship with Christ and His church. While writing this resource, I talked to many grieving mothers and fathers who bared their souls as they described the anguish of having a child far from God.

Randy and I taught two classes at a family conference using this resource. We titled the classes "Calling a Loved One Back to God." In each session we asked our guests to write on an index card the first name and situation of loved ones who were far from Christ. We then asked them to turn in the cards after class so that our staff could pray for them. The heartache they shared on those cards astounded us.

Approximately 50 attendees of our classes wrote down the names of 70 people who had strayed from the Father's love. Some of the quotes included:

"My sister has been through two marriages. She's bitter towards life and her heart is hard."

"My father-in-law was at one time an elder but has left the church because of his bitterness towards a feuding leadership."

"My Mom and Dad, who brought me up to know Christ, have since turned their hearts away."

"My friend was once a faithful follower of Christ but is now involved in an alternative life-style."

These quotes expressed the anguish in the hearts of Christians with loved ones away from God. If you were to ask your church family to hand in cards with names of prodigals they knew, you'd undoubtedly discover similar distressing stories. You and I have some stories of our own.

Persisting in Prayer

Jesus understands our frustrations and addresses the temptation we all face to give up on those close to us who have turned away from Him. He reaches out His hand and calls us to never quit praying.

In Luke 18, Jesus tells of the persistent widow who repeatedly came to a judge, crying out, "Grant me justice against my adversary." Though he had no fear of God, this man gave the widow her wishes because of her perseverance. Jesus is not saying that God is an unjust judge. However, He is saying that the Lord is One who honors the consistent pleas of His children. Jesus concludes this short parable with a promise...and then a probing question: "I tell you, he will see that they get justice, and quickly. However, when the Son of Man comes, will he find faith on the earth?"[4]

I believe that through this parable the Lord is telling us that when we face closed doors of frustration, to keep trusting Him, believing deep in our heart that He will come through with His promises. If this woman repeatedly approached this pagan judge with her pleas, can we not continue knocking on the Lord's door with trusting hearts?

Jesus can identify with all of us who have someone we love away from the loving touch of the Heavenly Father. He has millions of prodigal children. And He offers us an ever-flowing river of motivation and power not to give up on our loved ones.

The Change Within

One subtle aspect of persevering prayer is that as we continue to intercede, often through tears and great frustration, God changes us. The person for whom we're praying may not have yet changed, but we can. Some of the greatest work of the Holy Spirit is done in the lives of those walking in the furnace of persevering prayer. As we plead with Jesus to bring to Himself those we know and love, He will draw us to a more intimate love relationship.

There are certain people close to me who have been on my prayer list for many years. They are still not living for Christ.

Some mornings I feel called by God to fast and pray for them. One time when I was on vacation with a few of them, the Lord taught me a very important lesson.

Day by day our conversation covered nearly every topic but God. The One most important to me was of no interest to them. One night I got so frustrated with their lack of interest that I went to bed very angry. As I woke up the next morning, God convicted me to choose another path rather than the road of anger and self-righteousness. It was time instead to walk down the trail of intercessory prayer. Resisting my desire to eat a big breakfast, I decided to pray and fast throughout the morning, asking God to draw these people I loved into a relationship with Him. God transformed my attitude that morning. The Lord replaced my frustration with a concern for each of their souls.

In being forced to persevere in my intercession for those I love who are away from Christ, God changed me—to be more prayerful and to turn my loved ones over to Him. He reminded me of my weakness and inadequacy in bringing others to Him.

I once interviewed a father whose daughter had been away from God for many years. I asked him, "What was one of the best things you did while she was away?" He promptly answered, "Taking care of myself spiritually." He continued his answer with further wise counsel:

> If we put our life on pause until our child comes back, we're wasting our time. It's vital that we seek a close relationship with the Lord. My wife and I are learning to trust in God more, and even laugh more, rather than worrying about our child and her problems. We pray, turn the matter over to God and trust. Trusting God is the key. I'm learning to rest on God's

promises and to allow this parenting crisis to help me get closer to Him every day.

A Year of Homecoming

You may be wondering how your church could implement a congregation-wide effort to call prodigals home to God. Perhaps the story of how one church reached out to friends and family members in their community will give you some ideas.

A few months ago, a man named Ken Delano called me at my office. He is the involvement minister of the Darby Drive church in Florence, Alabama. He told of his excitement about a new project in their church, spawned by the use of our "Homecoming" kit. After viewing the videos in their Bible classes, the elders and staff set a bold goal for outreach. For the remainder of the year they planned to focus upon reaching out in love to the many delinquent members of Christ's body in their area.

This fired-up group of believers conducted a 24-hour prayer vigil. They kept their building open throughout the night, allowing members to come at any time to intercede on behalf of those they knew who had strayed from Christ. The leaders compiled a list of 185 people who had disconnected themselves from the Darby Drive family. Several members met in small groups and prayed by name for each one of these 185 souls. Within a few weeks this church joyfully witnessed God answering their prayers. Former members of their church began to come back to the fellowship. One of the returning families brought with them another family from the Florence community.

For the next several months this church continued a homecoming focus. Earlier this year I had the privilege of spending a weekend with this sweet gathering of believers. On Saturday night we met in Ken's home and prayed for many people in their community who were far from God. Sunday morning I spoke on a special Homecoming Day, urging visitors to receive God's grace and forgiveness, returning to their first love.

If your church knows of many prodigals in your city that were once an active part of your fellowship or any Christian fellowship, Darby Drive's story may inspire you to do likewise. Your congregation could sponsor events on weekends or Sundays where the primary thrust would be to call loved ones back to God.

A Prayer for Steadfastness

Right now I'm praying for those of you who are waiting for your own prodigals to return home to Jesus and His church family. I'm also begging the Lord to give your church patience, persistence and bold love as you pray for the spiritually homeless to return to Jesus. For you and your church, I pray this prayer of Paul's: "May the Master take you by the hand and lead you along the path of God's love and Christ's endurance."[5]

I realize it's hard to continue persevering in prayer. Waiting. Trusting. At times doubting. And wondering whether your prayers will ever make a difference in changing the hearts of that lost friend or child or spouse. I've been there. I'm still prayerfully waiting for those very close to me to bow their knee to Jesus. Last night I heard a very moving testimony at our church that has encouraged me to stay on my knees for those I love. I believe this story will touch your heart also.

Lost and Found

I couldn't think of a more terrifying experience than having one of my children run away from home and be missing for several days. Three years ago one teenage boy at our church disappeared. Last night he told his church family the entire story.

In October of 1997, this young man I'll call David abruptly left school in his pickup truck. He stole some money from a friend and headed out of town on a northbound highway. By midnight he reached Bryce City, Oklahoma, where he spent a lonely night in a cheap motel. He cried for much of the night. Back home his mother filed a missing person report with the police.

Late the next day this young fugitive pulled into a fast food restaurant in Denver, where, despite the knot in his stomach, he attempted to gulp down a chicken sandwich. He was frightened and lonely, but reluctant to call home.

That evening his family and many of their friends held a solemn prayer vigil in their home. Glenn Owen, one of our elders and a mentor to David, prayed a very specific prayer. He asked the Lord to cause the boy's truck to break down. Later that night, David heard a loud snapping noise as he entered Cheyenne, Wyoming. He was forced to pull into a repair shop to repair a broken alternator belt. The Father was watching over the lost son.

While flying home from a business trip to Florida, David's father pleaded with the Lord to provide a family to care for his son. God faithfully answered his prayers through a kind elderly couple named the Buttricks. This couple's son, Matt, met David at the service station where the truck was being repaired. Matt invited David to stay with his family. Unaware that this boy was only 15 and a runaway, this compassionate family took him in, putting him to work on their farm.

Each night as David's parents and hundreds of his brothers and sisters in Christ prayed for his safe return, he felt God working on his heart. Jesus Christ became very real to Him. "God worked miracles in my life each night," he told us. "Christ strengthened me."

Christ also gave strength to David's parents as they prayed and searched and waited. Finally, their agonizing 40-day vigil ended abruptly and mercifully.

The daughter of the Buttrick family happened to see a newscast describing David's disappearance. She immediately called the sheriff, who rushed to the Buttrick home to retrieve the boy. Within an hour David was in a youth detention center, awaiting a call from his parents. When both his parents called, only a few words could come out before they all began to sob. For six weeks David's parents had feared the worst, but prayed for the best. By God's tender mercy, the lost son was found. And he was very eager to come home.

The next day David walked with his mother into the living room of his home. He was overwhelmed by the sight of his family and friends awaiting him. Not with condemnation, but unconditional love. A few hours later his father arrived, having flown back from Canada where he had been searching for his lost son. Their embrace seemed to last a lifetime.

As David looked out on all of us while concluding his message, he said: "Without a mighty and gracious and forgiving God, I would not be here tonight. Without your prayers, I wouldn't be here. I'm a living testimony of all your prayers... and I love you for what you've done for me." He closed with this word from the Lord: "The LORD is far from the wicked but he hears the prayer of the righteous."[6]

Whenever I read that Proverb, I'll always be reminded of David's testimony—the power of a parent's prayer... and the wonder of a church united in prayer. Though we may have to wait a long time, and need to trust God's sovereignty for how

He will answer our heart's cry, we can be assured of this truth: our Lord does hear the prayers of the righteous.

Keep on Knocking

May we never stop praying and waiting and searching for that "missing person" who is away from the family of God. God hasn't given up on him or her. He is a Father who eagerly waits for His lost children to come home.

Stay on your knees. Continue knocking on that door. Tie those yellow ribbons around the trees. Prepare for the celebration. There may be a homecoming just around the corner. And what a festive occasion it will be.

Notes

1. Mark 9:24

2. Mark 9:29

3. William Hanford, "Help My Unbelief!," *Pray!*, Issue 16, 2000, 30-31.

4. Luke 18:1-8

5. 1 Thessalonians 3:5, *The Message*, translated by Eugene H. Peterson (Colorado Springs, CO: NavPress, 1993), 437.

6. Proverbs 15:29

Eight

The Overlooked Prayer Force

As we survey today's desolate society, some signs of hope and new life can be spotted on the horizon—in the vibrancy and passion of Christian youth.

Doug Tegner

An unexpected visitor dropped by our office recently. He's much younger than most others who come by to see us. Adam Lott is in the eighth grade and yet is far beyond his years in spiritual maturity. A week earlier Adam had accompanied his parents and older sister to a Monday night evangelism seminar hosted by our ministry. During the small group sessions, we shared with each other the first names of those who needed prayer for salvation. Adam eagerly told his group about lost friends whom he wanted to lead to Jesus. He knew of several kids at his middle school who were taking drugs. Adam's burning passion is that his peers be freed from the bondage of drugs through a relationship with the living God.

Two days after our seminar, Adam and his mother arrived at our office late Wednesday afternoon. They came to tell us how the Lord placed a dream in Adam's heart—to launch a Bible study at his school. He had already recruited a few Christians to begin meeting after school for prayer and Bible study. They hoped to invite their friends to join them. My cup was running over as I joined with his mother in laying hands on Adam, asking God's anointing upon him in this bold step of faith.

As I thought more about the visit from this young evangelist, I was overcome with awe at how the Lord works in such unusual ways. Our Monday night evangelism seminar was designed primarily to equip mature adults with tools to lead others to Christ. It was days later that God reminded me that He had some additional plans in mind—to plant the seed of evangelism in the heart of a teenager. Adam's visit was a sign to me from God of how powerfully He can work through young men and women.

Young People and Church Renewal

If you were to review the history of revivals among Christians in the past few centuries, what names would rise to the surface of your memory? We may think that the primary change agents in the church have been wise and seasoned leaders such as Martin Luther, John Wesley and Jonathan Edwards. However, if we would look back on some of the turning points in the life of the church, we'd be surprised to read of the many youthful leaders involved. Young followers of Jesus with a willing heart and strong faith in the living God have been mighty tools in His hands. Consider a few examples:

1. A teenager in Germany named Nicolas von Zinzendorf, age 16, joined with five other teenagers to form a school prayer group in the 1720's. This prayer group grew into a revival prayer movement that swept Europe.

2. In the U.S., two student prayer groups—one in 1806 and one in 1886—launched sweeping renewal movements. One revival led to nearly 20,000 praying youth whom God propelled into mission work over a 30-year period.

3. A 16-year-old girl in South Africa began a revival prayer meeting in 1860. The meeting grew so rapidly that it intimidated the famous preacher, Andrew Murray. At first he attempted to stop the meetings, but eventually repented of his fears and blindness. Murray went on to become one of the most influential writers on prayer and revival, writing more than 120 books.

4. Campus Crusade for Christ, one of the largest evangelistic ministries in our world today, was born in a 24-hour prayer vigil at UCLA.

5. Youth for Christ is rooted in the days when its only full-time staff member joined with others to preach all day and pray all night. His name was Billy Graham.

The Hunger for a New Work of God

Why is it that young people are often more receptive to spiritual renewal? While over forty adults attended our evangelism seminar, it was a thirteen-year-old middle school student who promptly launched a Bible study to reach his unsaved friends. We adults, who are so "wise" and experienced, failed to respond in such a spontaneous way in sharing our faith. David Bryant points to at least one reason for the openness of youth to the Spirit of God:

> Teens hold fewer presuppositions and prejudices against the notion that God can work in extraordinary ways. They have placed fewer boundaries on what they expect God to do. And they are often more aware of their brokenness than adults and more willing to admit they need a new work of God in their lives.[1]

Some recent events in my life have confirmed to me how many Christian young people today have a zeal for God and thus are boldly witnessing for Jesus.

Teens Making Church History Today

In the past few years, the biggest news regarding our high school campuses is the disturbing rise of violence. Shootings in Padukah and Littleton strike terror in the hearts of parents who have school-age children. Thankfully, in the midst of the dark forces invading our schools there's a much quieter and yet more powerful Presence at work. Student-led revival is permeating hundreds of our schools.

On the third Wednesday of each September, as parents drop off their children at school, they'll likely notice the crowds surrounding the flagpole. They're a part of the growing movement titled, "See You at the Pole." This movement burst spontaneously from a Dallas youth group and has swiftly spread to many other schools. The number of teens now meeting annually at school flagpoles has swelled to over three million teenagers taking a stand for Jesus Christ.

Thousands of Bible-study clubs and small groups have mushroomed throughout our nation's schools, led by students with a love for Jesus. They pray in triplets and engage in prayer-walks around the campus. As they stand at their lockers, they intercede for classmates whose lockers are adjacent to theirs.[2]

On the first few days of this school year, when I dropped off my son at our local high school, I noticed a sign of this spiritual fervor. Though the designated day for "See You at the Pole" had not yet arrived, many students had already begun praying. As I pulled away from the campus, I noticed a dozen or so students with hands clasped, singing and praying to the Lord around the flagpole. God is at work among our youth.

A Week of Revival

I love being in the presence of Christian young people who have a burning zeal for Jesus. In the last ten years, God has blessed my family with the opportunity to live near many such college students. We live less than a mile from the campus of Abilene Christian University. Since my wife teaches social work on that campus, she and I have had the privilege of opening our home to many of these college students. Their exuberance about life refreshes us. Those who are on fire for Christ especially invigorate our faith. Occasionally, I receive opportunities to speak to these students. One particular teaching moment stands out in my memory.

Two years ago a professor at this university invited me to teach his class on the topic of prayer and evangelism. I shared with them several examples from Scripture on ways that God faithfully responds to our intercession for lost souls. My greatest desire was to offer them, not so much information on the role of prayer in evangelism, but a dream—to reach many of their unsaved or lukewarm fellow students through fervent prayer.

I cast this vision to the class: to organize a weeklong prayer vigil for the campus during the spring semester. It would entail a week of focused prayer, asking God to work mightily among the students, staff and faculty. I invited students who were willing to help plan such a vigil to meet me after class. As the class ended, three students walked up to me and stated their willingness to implement this dream. The wheels of a campus-wide prayer revival had begun to turn.

In the next few weeks the four of us met, joined by the spiritual life director of the campus. As I helped them map out a week of prayer, I was overjoyed with their enthusiasm and fresh ideas. They planned a special prayer focus for each day of the week—one day designated to pray for lost students; another day dedicated to asking God to heat up the faith of lukewarm students. Other days were centered on repentance, the faculty and staff, and special prayers for students who were hurting and lonely.

These eager young leaders set up two prayer rooms on campus, where students could spend time alone with the Lord and write their requests on cards to leave in a box. As the week of prayer arrived, the boxes were filled with requests. Throughout the week, "prayer squads" visited the various offices of the faculty and staff. They gently gathered teachers and administrators together to spend a few moments thanking God for them and asking the Lord to grant them joy and energy in their kingdom work.

God took a handful of students who caught a dream for spiritual renewal and spread a blanket of His presence upon this campus. When God captures the hearts of young people, He can do some amazing things.

Much Activity...But Little Prayer

In the mid-1970's, during my first few years as a Christian, the Lord gave me a wonderful yet challenging experience. It was my first volunteer work in a local church. This small congregation in Southern California was in great need of someone with energy and zeal to lead their teenagers. In my enthusiasm, mixed with naiveté, I plunged into this work. A small band of junior high and high school kids seemed eager to get more involved in their church. God gave me the awesome task of uniting these teens into a rag-tag group of zealous believers. In spite of my inexperience and biblical illiteracy, I exerted by God's grace some positive influence on this youth group. Those days were filled with many joys, as well as some deep frustrations.

As I sit in my office, reflecting upon those adventurous days of youth leadership, I notice on my shelf a large leather-bound study Bible. It was a gift from this youth group on my twenty-seventh birthday. Knowing that I was planning to leave California and move to Dallas, this tenderhearted group of teens planned a surprise birthday for me. The capstone of the party was when they handed me this gift of God's word.

Pulling the Bible off the shelf and opening to the front cover, I read the names of many of these kids that I once helped shepherd—Michelle, Rachel, Dana, Blake and Art. Inscribed above their signatures is this note of appreciation: "This Bible... can't even begin to express our appreciation to you. You've been someone very special in all our lives and we'll miss you a lot. Please don't forget us! We love you always, the Camarillo Youth Group."

I certainly haven't forgotten these kids who occasionally broke my heart but ultimately stole it. Though I feel that many of the things I did with them were helpful in their spiritual formation, there was one key element that I sadly overlooked—preparing them to be prayer warriors. If the Lord gave me the opportunity to re-live those 27 months of training young disciples, I would re-direct my efforts. My primary agenda would be to pray for them, pray with them and call them to be agents of revival in their schools and church. I'd help them tap into the power of Christ, so He would release within them their great potential as mighty intercessors for God.

Calling Our Youth to Prayerful Renewal

If God has placed you in any sort of leadership position in the church, especially if it involves youth ministry, you can avoid the mistake I made as a novice church leader. The Lord has entrusted you with young people in your church who could be your greatest forces in prayer. There is spiritual dynamite in your congregation, just waiting for God to light the fuse. Perhaps there are only two or three teenagers who would catch the dream to be an instrument of revival. Even one teen is enough to spark revival. Recall the sixteen-year-old girl in South Africa. There may be such a girl in your church. I'm convinced that many of our teens in the church are waiting for someone to call them to launch out in faith and be bold instruments in God's hands.

Let me challenge you to begin praying for God to ignite a mighty renewal of the Spirit among the middle school, high school and college students in your congregation. To those of you in leadership positions in your church, let me be very direct: Are you willing to trust God so much that you'll let go of your desire to stay in control? God is in charge of the body of Christ—not you, not me. Christ's church doesn't belong to the leaders, but to Jesus. Let's allow God to be God, and allow the Holy Spirit to lead our congregations. Don't give in to fear. Trust God. Call your youth to seek revival. Then support them in their bold steps in prayer and outreach.

What if you and other church leaders began to host prayer times where you would target the hearts of the youth in your church? Traditionally, our prayers for young people often focus on asking God to help them stay pure and avoid sin. That's vital and I thank God for such prayers. But I'm calling us to go a step further.

I recommend that church leaders begin asking the Lord to use the youth in our communities of faith to show us as adults how to live more passionately for Jesus. I would love to hear of more shepherds doing what some of my church's leaders did last year with the middle and high school students.

On a Sunday evening last fall, a panel of church leaders conducted a dialogue with our auditorium class. The topic of the session was how parents can pass on their faith in Christ to our children. Near the end of the session, we broke up into groups to go to the youth classes and pray for them. My son told me later that he was deeply touched when several shepherds and their wives walked into his high school class and formed a circle around the students. Laying hands on these young disciples, they prayed God's blessing on them in the new school year. That evening, the adults gave our children one of the greatest gifts one could bestow on a person—the gift of intercessory prayer.

Five Smooth Stones...and a Childlike Faith

One of the most inspiring stories of the Old Testament is of a young boy with a deep trust in Almighty God. The sight of young David squaring off with the giant, Goliath, must have been nearly comical. He was a mere shepherd boy, armed with a sling shot and a few stones. Facing the mammoth, arrogant warrior Goliath must have been petrifying—from a human point of view. While Saul and the experienced army of Israel trembled as they heard Goliath's threats, David looked at this behemoth with a different set of eyes. By faith he claimed the promise that standing behind him was the creator of the universe. In bold trust he cried out to Goliath: "You come against me with sword and spear and javelin, but I come against you in the name of the LORD Almighty..."[3]

I believe there are many "Davids" among our congregations today—including the one who came into our office several weeks ago. They are prepared to slay giants.

I can still picture that scene in our office foyer, as we laid hands on Adam, the thirteen-year-old evangelist. We pleaded with the Lord to fulfill this young man's dream to reach his lost classmates. By his own effort, Adam doesn't have much of a chance in bringing his peers to Christ. In God's strength, however, he is becoming an awesome tool in the hands of Jesus.

The Unfolding Dream

One morning at my office I began wondering how Adam's dreams were unfolding. In the Lord's beautiful timing, an e-mail arriving later that morning made this story even richer. Adam's mother, Laurie, had some news she couldn't resist telling me. She reminded me that Adam had started his Bible study at his middle school during the final weeks of school last year. Then came the big news: his group has now decided to conduct this study during lunch every day this year!

Laurie went on to describe how her family senses the Lord calling them to embark upon a weekly evangelistic Bible study in their home. They're allowing their children and fellow students to lead the study. They also plan to attend our next evangelism seminar and hope to bring with them many teenagers. The story of David slaying the giant continues to repeat itself. Thank You, Lord, for how you lead us through the zeal of these Christian teens.

As you and I call our youth to bold faith and fervent prayer, we'll likely see more giants fall. May we look to our young people as potentially the greatest prayer force of our churches. These young disciples of Christ may be the ones God will raise up to make new history in His church.

While we dream for ways the Lord could infuse the youth of our churches with His renewing power, join me in offering this prayer on their behalf:

> Father, I pray for a mighty anointing of Your Spirit upon each young person in our congregations. Forgive us for how we've sinned against You and them in not praying for them. Please teach us about zealous faith and passionate prayer through the example of our children. I plead with You to plant a seed in these students'

hearts—a seed of a fresh, new vision for ways Your kingdom can grow in dramatic ways through them. Then help us adults to get out of the way. In the Mighty Name of Jesus, Amen.

Notes

1. David Bryant, "Is This the Generation?," *Pray!*, Issue 8, September/October 1998, 10-11.

2. Doug Tegner, "Revival Stream in a Cultural Desert," *Pray!*, Issue 8, September/October 1998, 15.

3. 1 Samuel 17:45a

Nine

On Our Feet in Prayer

Talking to men for God is a great thing, but talking to God for men is greater still.

E. M. Bounds

What is the first image that comes to your mind when you think of praying? Being on your knees at your bedside? Saying grace as you gather around the dinner table with your family? Seated in a pew at church, bowing your head as someone leads a public prayer?

I'd like you to consider a somewhat unusual form of prayer: *prayerwalking*. It involves praying with your feet moving and your eyes wide open. Many Christians in our country are using this method to pray for the spiritual awakening of their neighborhoods. Others are prayerwalking in attempts to reach entire cities.

Steve Hawthorne defines prayerwalking as praying on site with insight. It's an uncomplicated plan where Christians walk in small groups in neighborhoods, praying for the residents of every house they pass. One of the great advantages of this method is that it brings pray-ers into the community.[1] Peter Wagner observes that any Christian can go on a prayerwalk.

It doesn't require a Bible degree or a gift of public speaking. Wagner writes: "They can be plain, everyday Christians who love the Lord and who believe that God is calling His people these days to not only pray for their community, but to pray in their community."[2]

Here are a few examples of prayerwalks conducted in a variety of locations:

One weekend a month, a team of pray-ers in Santo Domingo, Dominican Republic walks through the city parks and prays for three hours. Periodically, 400 people meet and pray in 10 groups of 40. They pray for one hour at certain intersections throughout their city.

In Savannah, New York, one minister called his church to canvass every home in that city. As they walked their neighborhoods, his church members avoided ringing doorbells or handing out literature. Instead, they prayed for every house they passed during their walks. After conducting prayerwalks for 25 weeks, the church witnessed some visible results. Newcomers began visiting the church's worship assemblies. On one Sunday four families from one street came to a Sunday morning service only a week after some Christians had walked and prayed in their neighborhood.

A Christian nurse used her break time to walk the halls of the hospital, praying for the patients and staff.[3]

One minister experienced a radical transformation in his life and his church when God opened his eyes to this new form of prayer. After working thirteen years with a church that had become increasingly embroiled in conflict, he witnessed a new emphasis in prayer and evangelism in his congregation. This prayer focus transformed the community as the church shifted from in-house battles to a consistent focus on prayerful outreach.

A Broader Vision of Prayer

Dee Duke serves as a minister for a small church in Oregon. Several years ago he attended a leadership conference that introduced him to the concept of prayerwalking. Returning to his church with a renewed vision for prayer, he confessed to his flock one Sunday that he had allowed prayer to slip to the bottom of his priorities. From that point onward he vowed to lead from his knees.

Duke's honest confession and revived passion for prayer inspired his congregation to follow in his steps. Several members of his congregation began sponsoring prayerwalks in their neighborhoods. On every prayerwalk leaders gave each participant refreshments and maps before sending them out to walk and pray. God began to do some amazing things through this church's prayers.

The church broadened their outreach in these walks. They mapped out a section of the town within several miles of their church. These zealous followers of Christ instituted a plan to systematically walk through every neighborhood of that area. On each walk they pleaded with God to draw lost souls to Himself. Eventually, this passion for prayer trickled down to the youth of the church. The young people developed an even broader strategy for prayerwalking.

One summer the youth group from Duke's church decided to travel to the four corners of Oregon and conduct prayer sessions at each of these locations. Their goal was to stand at each corner of the state and pray for the salvation of the lost, especially teenagers. This church's prayer outreach continued to expand.

When hearing a man speak at their church about his prayerwalk across the United States, these passionate believers caught another dream for prayer. They made plans to join

80 other churches and conduct a prayerwalk across the entire stretch of Highway 20, which runs throughout the state. I'm persuaded that many lost souls will be reached as a result of the efforts of this small church that is deeply committed to evangelism through prayerwalking.[4]

My Introduction to Prayerwalking

I recall vividly the first time I heard someone describe a prayerwalk. Two years ago my wife and I heard a woman named Jan tell a dramatic story. Her two brothers were scheduled to arrive in our city one summer, leaving their home on the East Coast. They were preparing to begin high school in the fall. Jan was burdened with the knowledge that her siblings had been heading down the path of sin. Knowing that their spiritual lives were in danger, she initiated a prayer strategy to pave the way for their arrival. Jan used some unusual prayer methods.

First, she wrote promises from Scripture on note cards and secretly taped them on the backside of the headboards of her brothers' beds. She asked the Lord to protect and guard their thought life while they slept in their beds.

Second, a few days before school was to begin, Jan went on a solo prayerwalk throughout her brothers' future high school. Her heart burned with the desire to cover in prayer every area of the school grounds. She stopped at strategic areas of the school to ask God's blessings upon her siblings. Jan's prayers touched nearly every square foot of the school.

Every time she drove near the high school, Jan circled around the campus, praying for the Lord to use godly teachers and peers to impact her brothers for Jesus. Yesterday I called Jan to get an update on her brothers. She told me how faithful God has been in honoring her prayers.

God led both of her brothers to several teachers who loved Christ. A few of the students whom Jan had taught years earlier at her church became influential peers to the two boys. Today one of her brothers is a senior at a Christian university. Though her other brother is not quite where Jan would like him to be, he is setting and reaching some good personal goals. And he is a much different young man from when he first arrived in our city. Jan's final words to me especially grabbed my attention: "If one of my brothers had not come here to school, he would probably be dead from drugs."

Inspired by Jan's prayers for her brothers, my wife and I have begun an annual tradition. On the first day of each school year, we slowly drive around both of our children's schools and pray for them. We ask God to protect Aaron and Shannon from evil and to provide them with Christian peers and positive teachers. We plead with the Lord to keep them safe from school violence and to use them both as spiritual influences on their campuses. A week prior to our son starting high school, my wife and I walked throughout the halls of his school, praying for the Lord to watch over Aaron throughout his school year. As I look back on these two years, I realize how God has answered our prayers for our children, especially in leading them to spiritually-minded friends.

Moving Into the Streets

Two years after hearing Jan speak, I experienced another kind of prayerwalking. This time it was a walk on behalf of those I didn't know.

One Wednesday night a half dozen of our church's prayer ministry gathered at an apartment complex a few blocks from our church building. Armed with several bookmarks with quotes from Jesus and a notepad for writing prayer requests, we went from door to door with a simple announcement—we were there to pray for each resident. The reaction of most people we met was very encouraging.

I remember Vernell. When he first answered our knock, he cracked open the door cautiously and looked at us with suspicion. When he realized we were there simply to pray for him, Vernell warmed up to us and asked that we pray for him to be admitted to truck driving school.

Our visit with William also stands out. He wore no shirt. His face was wrinkled with what appeared to be many years of hard living. Yet there was a sweetness to him that seemed to reveal his desire to get right with God. He admitted that he had made a commitment to Jesus many years ago, but had drifted away. Though he was anxious to get back to his dinner, William spent a few minutes talking with us and was grateful for our visit.

After knocking on every door of the complex, our team of pray-ers began a slow walk around the perimeter of the apartments. As we stepped towards the back of the complex, a foul smell emanating from the trash containers was overpowering. It was like a metaphor for the sin that held captive the lives of many of the apartment's residents.

We took turns praying out loud, asking God to bring His salvation to the adults of the apartments. The tail end of our walk brought us the greatest surprise. It was a true work of God.

Tony was seated in his lawn chair outside his apartment, having a beer with his buddy. As he saw us approaching, he seemed both embarrassed and delighted to see us. Before we said a word, Tony began confessing his sins to us. He cried out, "I know I shouldn't be drinking beer and smoking. All of my brothers and sisters are in church but me. Two of my brothers are preachers. I was baptized when I was 14, but I just can't seem to give up my beer. But I really appreciate what you all are doing."

Spontaneously two members of our prayer team told Tony that God loved him and wanted him to come home to the Lord. Carolyn, a leader in our prayerwalk, made her way over to Tony and handed him a bookmark with Scriptures on it. In her kind voice she assured him that Jesus loved him, saying, "Tony, when your entire family is begging you to come to Christ, don't you know that this is Jesus calling you? He wants you." Tony nodded his head and seemed to acknowledge that the Lord was in pursuit of him.

As our team said goodbye to him and continued around the block, we asked the Father to draw Tony into relationship with Him. Later that evening, as I drove away from the apartments, I was bathed in the afterglow of this simple and yet profound prayer experience. Six of us sacrificed only two hours to interact with people whom we might never have met had we not literally walked into their world. I saw first hand the effectiveness of prayerwalking. It draws Christians out of the comfort of their church buildings and into the lives of their neighbors. I needed the Lord to yank me out of my routine in order to pray for souls of people I could see face to face. I'm ready to go on another prayerwalk.

Prayerwalks and Prayerdrives

I urge you to call members of your church to conduct a prayerwalk. Try it one time and watch how the Lord blesses the experience. Perhaps only a handful of your congregation would be interested in this adventure of faith. Don't be discouraged if at first only a few people sign up for such an event. Remember that our Lord started with only twelve men. Choose a Wednesday evening or Sunday night and break the routine of your church meeting. Challenge those you know who have a heart for prayer to conduct a one or two hour prayerwalk. Announce the walk through an e-mail or a card in the mail. Then pray for the Lord to raise up men, women and children from your church to hear His call to walk and pray for lost souls.

Consider asking one or two volunteers to select certain areas of your city in which your group could walk and pray. When people arrive for the beginning of the walk, be prepared to hand them a map and brief instructions for where to go and what to do. Suggest that all of you go door to door, telling the residents that your purpose is simply to pray for them. Make sure they have a pad and pencil to write prayer requests when they meet people at the door. Have a brief prayer as a group and then disperse for an hour to walk and pray in your designated areas.

It's vital that we include elderly or handicapped believers in this effort. I recommend that you provide them this alternative: a "prayerdrive." They can drive slowly through a designated neighborhood, taking turns to pray for those who live in each house they pass. Prayerdrives can be effective alternatives to prayerwalks for everyone when the weather is too hot or cold.

At the conclusion of the hour, suggest that your teams return to your original meeting place to de-brief and give thanks to the Lord for how He worked among you. Discuss not only the response of the people for whom you offered prayer, but also how God changed you. I firmly believe that if you introduce even a few willing Christians to prayerwalking, it won't be their last one.

Those who do engage in this prayer experiment can expect at least two results. First, many of those participating will likely become more focused on outsiders. In my Wednesday night experience, God convicted me of how I dwell too often on my needs and problems. In those two hours He opened my eyes to the needs of many people who are trapped in sin and in desperate need of Jesus, the deliverer.

Second, God will begin acting on those for whom you pray. Expect some of these neighbors to begin showing some interest in Christ. A few of us who engaged in our recent prayerwalk plan to meet again to pray specifically for the apartment complex where we conducted the prayerwalk, asking God to break the strongholds of sin in the lives of those who are outside of Christ. By faith, we're expecting the Lord to dispel the spiritual darkness with the light of the gospel.

Called Into the World

Prayerwalks. An unusual idea. A simple method of prayer evangelism. An effective way for Christians to leave the security of their church meetings and actively pray for the souls of those near their home or church.

Anticipate a price to be paid for conducting prayerwalks. As Peter Wagner says, "The major cost for ministering to a neighborhood through prayerwalking is time."[5] Is your church ready to sacrifice some of its regular fellowship and study times for a walk or drive on behalf of the eternal welfare of your unbelieving neighbors? These efforts will take time. Yet they are well worth the hour or two break from our normal routine. In my brief experience, the prayerwalk was two of the richest and most productive hours spent for the sake of the kingdom.

I'm thinking again of Tony. I remember so well the conflict etched on his face and expressed in his confession. He was caught in the tension of seeking the pleasures of the world and yet miserable with the knowledge that his life was not right with God. Our prayerwalk was a visual reminder to him that Jesus wants him home. I'm praying for Tony to come home to the Lord soon.

Jesus calls us as His disciples to go into all the world rather than stay clustered safely in church buildings. I'm convinced that several members of our congregations would respond to the call of a prayerwalk or prayerdrive if we would challenge them to do it. The plan is simple. The call to make disciples is clear. Will we take hold of the challenge, periodically leaving our comfortable pews and getting on our feet in prayer? Jesus will be walking by our side. He's promised us that when we go into all the world, He will be with us. We won't walk alone. And consider this glorious possibility: those for whom we pray may one day join us on a walk—a walk right into the very gates of heaven.

Notes

1. Peter Wagner, *Churches That Pray* (Ventura, CA: Regal Books, 1993), 172.

2. Ibid.

3. Ibid., 174-175.

4. Dee Duke, "Putting Feet to Your Prayers," *Leadership*, Summer 2000, 100-101.

5. Wagner, *Churches That Pray*, 177.

Ten

Wrestling on Our Knees

*The great people of the earth today are the people who pray.
I do not mean those who talk about prayer; nor those who say
they believe in prayer...I mean those who take time and pray.*

S. D. Gordon

It was a frightening experience. My wife and I had never seen it happen to one of our children. It all began ten years ago when our son, Aaron, contracted the flu. Standing up to his strong will, we urged him to stay in bed throughout the weekend. On Sunday morning I went to church by myself while my wife stayed home with Aaron and our daughter, Shannon. It was an uneventful morning—until I arrived home from church.

As I walked into our front door, my wife rushed to meet me with these words: "You wouldn't believe what happened this morning. Aaron's fever shot up suddenly and he began to have a seizure." While I was enjoying worship at church, our house was filled with firemen and paramedics. It was a terrifying moment for Susan and our daughter as they witnessed this six-year old boy shake with convulsions. What a relief it was to us when the seizures stopped and the medical personnel felt it was safe to leave him.

The one incident that stands out for me that morning is when Aaron first began to have the seizure. Susan immediately turned to Shannon, who was three at the time, and said, "Start praying for your brother." This miniature prayer warrior promptly leaped up, ran to our bedroom, got on her knees and began praying for her big brother. Realizing Aaron was in danger, Shannon fervently prayed for God to heal him. She took prayer very seriously.

Throughout this chapter, I want you to keep before you that vivid image—our young daughter on her knees, pleading with God to take care of Aaron. Then imagine yourself kneeling by your bed, entering the throne room of God, and pleading on behalf of a person you love whose soul is endangered.

On His Knees Before God

Tucked away in the book of Colossians is the name of a man whom the apostle Paul held in high esteem. This man wasn't known necessarily for his great teaching. Paul didn't commend him for how he preached or for the many souls he won to Jesus Christ. His notoriety came not from how he stood before crowds and talked about the resurrected Lord, but how he knelt before the King of Kings and prayed for others.

His name was Epaphras. Paul mentions him three times. The apostle called him a faithful servant of Christ[1] and a fellow prisoner.[2] The description of this godly man that stands out to me in bold print is that he was known simply as a man who was "always wrestling in prayer" for others.[3]

Wrestling in prayer implies that there is a struggle involved. There is some sort of resistance from an opponent. I remember well my high school days when I would watch our Buena High School wrestling team compete against other schools. The matches were intense. Each contestant was acutely alert. On guard. Muscles tense. Each wrestler used every bit of his strength and training to pin his opponent…and to prevent himself from being pinned to the mat.

Epaphras' fellow prisoner wrote these words, describing the spiritual wrestling match in which we are engaged:

> God is strong and he wants you strong. So take everything the Master has set out for you, well-made weapons of the best materials. And put them to use so you will be able to stand up to everything the Devil throws your way. This is no afternoon athletic contest…This is for keeps, a life-or-death fight to the finish against the Devil and all his angels.[4]

I counted the word "against" six times in another translation of this verse. There is an enemy of our souls and his name is Satan. He hates when Christians unite in prayer, calling upon the mighty name of Jesus. He will do everything he can to distract us from a deep dependence upon the Lord. He is *against* us. Thankfully, One who is far more powerful than our enemy is for us.

One of Satan's greatest distractions to keep us from wrestling in prayer is to delude us into thinking that we're not involved in a war. The enemy is plotting against the church to lull her into a peacetime mentality.

A Weakened Military

Last year I was on a flight from Dallas to Huntsville, Alabama. Seated behind me were two men who became engaged in a very interesting conversation about our military. One of the men was a Vietnam veteran headed for a weekend reunion with his fellow vets. The other man was a civilian who worked with our country's defensive missile system. As their conversation deepened, they both agreed about the weakening condition of the United States' military. They grieved over the fact that thousands of talented men are bailing out of the armed forces in pursuit of more money in the private sector. The more these men talked, the more they were convincing each other that our nation is becoming more vulnerable to enemy attacks.

Reflecting on this conversation, I began to think of the danger of a peacetime mentality. It can occur in a country and too often takes place in a church. Satan blinds us from seeing the biblical truth that we're engaged in a spiritual conflict for people's souls. I forget this truth so quickly.

We forget until there's a wakeup call such as another high school shooting. Or another terrorist attack in Israel. Or another marriage at our church torn apart by divorce.

I'm sure that one of Epaphras' great motivations to "wrestle in prayer" was a keen awareness that believers are involved in an intense spiritual battle with the enemy of our souls. Satan means war—and so must God's people.

Neil Anderson tells the story of a man who had once been a high priest in the upper levels of Satanism. By God's grace he found Jesus and was dramatically delivered from the pit of spiritual darkness. Six months later he gave his testimony at Anderson's church. After he concluded his story, one person asked him a very important question based on his experience from the dark side: "What should the church's first line of defense be as Christians face demonic influences?" I read carefully his response: "Prayer," he answered forcefully. "And when you pray, mean it. Fervent prayer thwarts Satan's activity like nothing else." Anderson concluded: "God has...equipped you and authorized you for search and rescue in the lives of those who are in the devil's clutches."[5]

Someone Was Praying

As I think of those prayerful believers who have intersected my life, men and women who took very seriously this call to intercession, a few names come to mind:

A woman named Lynne recently told me of her grandfather who prayed for her before she was born. She keeps at home a treasured letter in which he wrote his prayer for the next three generations of his family—that they would all become Christians. God is graciously answering these prayers. The day she told me about this letter, her fourth son, Mark, confessed Jesus Christ as His Savior and Master at his baptism. A wonderful answer to the prayers of his grandfather, a man he'll someday meet in heaven.

My mother-in-law, Virginia Vaught, has taught me a great deal about prayer. She and her husband prayed for all five of their daughters to marry strong Christians. In His great mercy God has answered those hundreds of prayers. And by God's grace I became one of the benefactors of all those pleadings before the Lord. While I was caught in my sin for many years, my future in-laws were praying for me, though they had no idea who I was.

As I look back on my life the past 25 years, I can see the results of my in-laws' many prayers. Two years after my conversion to Christ, He led me to leave my home state of California and move to Dallas. There I met the woman I was to marry. In reflecting upon how I met my wife, it's clear that someone had been praying—Bill and Virginia Vaught.

A man named Rick spoke at a retreat I attended two years ago. Though he was raised in a Christian home, he went through a long period of sin during his college years. Eventually he came back to the Lord and is now very involved with his church. He said in his message, "I don't know why the Lord protected me when I had gotten into drugs and all sorts of immoral living while in college."

When Rick finished his talk, an older man came up to him and said, "Let me tell you a story. I knew your parents during your college years. I worked with each of them and I remember the agony they went through during your time of rebellion. They were constantly on their knees while you were caught up in sin. God heard their prayers and that's why you were protected." Someone was praying.

On His Knees For Us

The supreme example of someone wrestling in prayer is our Lord. Try to grasp the agony within His soul as Jesus went through inner torture on our behalf:

> During the days of Jesus' life on earth, he offered up prayers and petitions with loud cries and tears to the one who could save him from death, and he was heard because of his reverent submission. Although he was a son, he learned obedience from what he suffered and, once made perfect, he became the source of eternal salvation for all who obey him.[6]

Jesus suffered tremendously for us in order to save us. Imagine the agony He endured on our behalf while in the garden of Gethsemane. Try to grasp the immense burden on His shoulders as He anticipated the horror of the cross.

Our Lord calls those He saves to wrestle in prayer on behalf of others—that the lost might be saved and the saved might be strengthened and persevere in their faith.

Becoming an Epaphras

What will wake us up and inspire us to become like an Epaphras and begin wrestling in prayer on behalf of others? Let me offer a way to start.

Several months ago I spoke on this subject on a Wednesday night. At the end of my message, I asked the congregation to write on a card the first name of those for whom they wanted to pray—for salvation, healing, marriage restoration. At the end of the evening, I asked them to bring their prayer card forward. Many people came to me afterwards to hand me their card. I assured them that others would pray for these matters that burned in their hearts. There was a look of gratitude in their eyes as they seemed reassured that other believers would be joining them in praying for this burden on their hearts.

I encourage you to take some time at your church to engage in a focused session of wrestling in prayer for those who are in deep need of God's intervention. You might do this one Sunday during the morning worship. Perhaps your small group or Bible class could spend an hour writing names on index cards, praying for them during that hour and committing to continue praying the next week. When you come back together, you could report on how you saw the Lord work in their lives.

Kneeling Humbly Before God

The image of our daughter flashes back into my mind. I can see this three-year-old girl, pleading with God to heal her big brother. What Shannon did for her brother has taught me much about what we as adults can do for others—going humbly before our God to intervene in another person's life.

Very few people knew what Shannon had done that morning—initially, only my wife and our son. This news didn't make the local paper. No television crew came by the house to film it. Her prayer was very private. However, Someone saw what she was doing...and He answered her prayer.

As I reflect more about Shannon's example of spontaneous prayer, I'm thinking that the place to begin a prayer ministry is in the prayer closet. If God is placing on your heart right now to be a part of a church that truly wrestles in prayer for others, He may be calling you to engage in a great deal of private prayer. It could be that He is leading you to a season of behind-the-scenes prayer for your church, your family, and friends. There will be no fanfare. No one is going to host a large banquet in your honor. And yet as with my daughter, so with you—Someone will hear your prayers. And He will respond.

In these times of quiet intercession, cling tenaciously to this promise from our Lord: "But when you pray, go into your room, close the door and pray to your Father, who is unseen. Then your Father, who sees what is done in secret, will reward you."[7]

Claim that promise as you agonize in prayer for others: Your Father will see you in secret and will reward you. Count on it.

Thirty Years of Prayer

Hundreds of years ago, there lived a man who rebelled against God for several years. He was a brilliant intellectual who wasted much time in the wilderness of sin. Yet, throughout that time, God pursued him. And a mother prayed continually for him.

Finally, after studying the Christian faith, Augustine Aurelius stopped running from God. He came to faith in Christ and surrendered his life to Him. Augustine went on to become one of the most influential Christian thinkers in the history of the church. From the eighth through the twelfth centuries, his works were read more than any other author. Malcolm Muggeridge summarizes the influence of this great theologian: "Thanks largely to Augustine, the light of the New Testament did not go out with Rome's, but remained amidst the debris of the fallen empire to light the way to another civilization, Christendom."[8]

Millions of Christians have been influenced by Augustine's writings. However, very few know about his mother, Monica. They may not realize that this godly woman prayed fervently for her son for thirty years, begging God to bring him to salvation. The day finally came. Her prayers were finally answered. Not long after Augustine's conversion, Monica told her son that her mission in life had been accomplished. She had seen him come to faith in Christ, and when she left this world, she died in peace.[9]

Staying on our knees for someone else is hard work. It can be discouraging. If we need to wait for years for God to answer our prayers, it can be wearisome and testing to our faith. Yet the Lord will reward our times of wrestling in prayer—in ways we may not see until we get to heaven.

God hasn't given up on His wandering children. He continues pursuing them, right to the end. May we do the same for others, as we follow Him on our knees.

Notes

1. Colossians 1:17

2. Philemon 1:23

3. Colossians 4:12

4. Ephesians 6:10-12, *The Message*, translated by Eugene H. Peterson (Colorado Springs, CO: NavPress, 1993), 410.

5. Neil Anderson, *The Bondage Breaker* (Eugene, Oregon: Harvest Publishers, 1993), 86, 91.

6. Hebrews 5:7-9

7. Matthew 6:6

8. Malcolm Muggeridge, *A Third Testament* (Boston: Little, Brown, 1976), 29.

9. Ruth Bell Graham, *Prodigals and Those Who Love Them* (Colorado Springs, CO: Focus on the Family Publishing, 1991), 3, 10.

Eleven

A Baptism of Compassion

*Let my heart be broken with the things that break
the heart of God.*

Bob Pierce

Our sixteen-year-old son, Aaron, has a passion for golf. For
the past four years he's spent the majority of his waking
hours on a golf course. Last year he joined the high school golf
team. Nearly every afternoon he's out on the course or the
range working on his game. He reads golf magazines. Takes
lessons. And nearly every weekend he's watching a golf tour-
nament on television (most often with his Dad).

The Power of Passion

What is it about passion that drives people and consumes
them with excelling in a sport, building a business or raising a
family? Think of all the countries explored, the sports records
broken, and companies founded as a result of passion. This
force works like a high-powered engine that drives men and
women to accomplish lofty goals.

Ponder for a moment another kind of passion. A passion
that is deep within the heart of God. It's a longing to bring His

lost children home. Consider our Savior's single-minded devotion to the Father's will as He walked this earth, headed straight to the cross. One man who had the privilege of walking with the Savior for three years describes the passion our Lord has for lost people: "God...is restraining himself on account of you, holding back the End because he doesn't want anyone lost. He's giving everyone space and time to change."[1]

At times God needs to break our hearts in order to give us this similar passion for reaching the unsaved. One story I read recently describes this experience well.

Tears of Compassion

Bruce Marciano is a Hollywood actor who is deeply committed to Christ. God once blessed him with the wonderful opportunity to portray Jesus in a series of videos based on the book of Matthew. His portrayal of our Master is my favorite. Based on this experience, Bruce wrote a soul-gripping book titled *In the Footsteps of Jesus.* He describes how the Lord worked in amazing ways before, during and after the production.

One story that particularly moved me is his description of the scene based on the incident in Matthew 11 where Jesus declared woes over the sins of unrepentant cities. Filming this scene became one of the most touching moments in Bruce's acting career.

On the morning of the shooting, Bruce was deep in prayer while preparing to act in the scene. With extras and camera crew milling around him, Bruce whispered, "Lord, show me what it all looks like through Your eyes." Then this picture flashed in his mind—a sea of people drowning in sin. He saw men and women who were far from God's love and outside of His goodness and plans for them. Bruce's body began shaking as this vision from God flooded his soul. A verse of Scripture came to his mind: "When he saw the crowds, he had compassion on them, because they were harassed and helpless, like sheep without a shepherd."[2] Bruce suddenly realized that when Jesus cried out, "Woe to you, Korazin! Woe to you, Bethsaida!" he did so with a broken heart. "It was the desperate scream of a parent watching his own child step off a curb in front of a moving car."[3]

I want Jesus to give me that kind of perspective. I desperately need the Lord to break through my selfishness, pride and judgmental spirit. To let Christ replace my self-centered agenda with a deep, passionate concern for those outside the protective covering of our Lord.

A Baptism of Compassion

Evangelist and writer Ed Silvoso describes some thrilling events among churches today that are attempting to influence entire cities for Christ. One story he told captures a way to see people as God sees them.

Silvoso experienced a dramatic conversion to Christ as a teenager, and immediately became very zealous in sharing Christ with the lost. Whenever he saw a funeral procession, he wondered whether that person had gone to heaven or hell. His fervor in sharing Jesus with others was all-consuming:

> I was terribly afraid that one of my friends, family members or classmates would die and go to hell! I knew that God wanted all of them to be saved, and I wanted to please the One who had saved me. When one of my friends fell fatally ill, I barged into the room where he was confined, and I led him to Christ just hours before he died.[4]

But over time Silvoso's evangelistic fire gradually diminished. As he attended college and seminary, his intellectual training led him to become less enamored with God's love for him and for those without the Savior. Then one day the Lord shattered his complacency when he read 2 Peter 3:9: "The Lord is not slow in keeping his promise, as some understand slowness. He is patient with you, not wanting anyone to perish, but everyone to come to repentance."

He described the moment as if the Lord had hit him with a two-by-four: "I fell on my knees and cried out to God for a baptism of compassion for the lost. As I repented of my spiritual complacency, God's grace washed away the apathy...God's love flooded my soul and restored the joy of my salvation."[5]

Brought to My Knees

The Lord also hit me with a two-by-four. Silvoso's story quickly triggered memories of my early days of walking with Jesus. My mind raced back to my conversion 24 years ago. A few weeks after Christ turned my life around, I began waiting tables at a restaurant. Most of my co-workers were caught in the trap of Satan, seeking the pleasures of the world. I eagerly sought ways to share my faith with them and attempted to live before them an example of Christ-likeness.

The following year my church offered me an opportunity to correspond with men and women in Africa who were enrolled in Bible studies. I plunged into this work, excited about being an "overseas missionary" by mail. But this zeal didn't last.

Three years after Christ delivered me from sin, He gave me the privilege of attending a Bible school. I later went to graduate school, where I engaged in further studies in Bible and ministry. While I'm extremely thankful for my theological training, I can now see that something slowly changed within me during those years. My training for ministry gradually became a quest for learning the Bible as an end in itself, rather than as a way to share Christ more effectively with others. Simultaneously, my child-like faith and sense of urgency in reaching those without Christ diminished.

The similarities between Silvoso's story and mine struck me. I put his book down, got down on my knees in my office and repented of my lack of love for the lost. I prayed that the Lord would give me a baptism of compassion for those who don't know Jesus. Within an hour I sensed my heart being transformed. God was already answering my prayer.

While running errands during my lunch hour that day, I caught myself looking differently at the store clerks. God had heightened my awareness that these weren't merely clerks to meet people's needs. They were precious souls for whom Jesus died. The Lord had given me a baptism of compassion. Now I realize that each day I need the Lord to renew my mind and grant me a sensitive, caring passion for the lost.

Golfing For Jesus

One man I know has such a white-hot passion for sharing his hope in Christ with people he meets each day. Milton Jones has been a minister in Seattle for the past two decades. He describes his evangelistic focus as "putting in a good word for Jesus." Last year he spoke at a conference on how to share one's faith with non-believers. One story he told reveals his great passion for relating the gospel to those who intersect his life.

Milton shares my son's love for golf. Whenever his schedule is open, he rounds up a foursome of friends to play 18 holes. One day he arrived at the course and realized that his group needed one more player. The pro shop at the course assigned to them a recent college graduate named James. For the first few holes Milton simply enjoyed the company and concentrated on his golf game. However, God had other plans.

By the time he finished the ninth hole, Milton sensed the Lord prompting him to "put in a good word for Jesus." The prompting was continuous. Within a few minutes he took the plunge and decided to initiate a conversation with James. At first their words consisted of small talk as James mentioned that he had once played football for the University of Washington. Then Milton dove in with his word for Jesus.

He said, "James, I've worked for years on that campus. In fact, I have recently led a Bible study for the football team. I'm surprised our paths didn't cross. There is only one reason that I moved to Seattle. I came here to tell people about Jesus. James, do you know Jesus?"

James paused for a moment and then responded honestly, "No, I don't. I really don't. Not like I think you're talking about." When Milton invited James to church, he received a surprise response. James showed up the next Sunday, loved the worship and was moved by the friendliness of the people there.

At first Milton was excited about how the Lord used him to tell a stranger about Jesus. But his excitement was quickly extinguished. The next Sunday James wasn't there—and he never came to that church again. Milton later learned that James received a job offer and had left Seattle. It was a great disappointment. Milton lamented to the Lord, "God, what are you doing? I told James about Jesus and then You moved him away."

It would be two years before Milton would see how the Lord had used his words on the golf course. One Saturday evening he received a call at home. It was James, who had some great news to announce. "Milton, I called you because I thought you'd want to know what's going to happen in the morning. I've been going to church and I plan to be baptized tomorrow." James ended the phone conversation with words that Milton will likely never forget: "I would not have become a Christian if you hadn't talked to me on the golf course that day."[6]

I desperately long for the type of passion Milton has to lead others to Jesus. I know it doesn't come naturally. I'm too self-centered. It must be derived from above. As we ask the Lord to give us a "baptism of compassion" for the lost, we can count on Him doing it.

A Church in Repentance

One of the most powerful ways to experience such a renewal of the heart is for a group of believers in Christ to cry out together for God to change them. Great things can happen when we as God's people repent of our self-centeredness, prejudice and lack of love for others. God moves mightily when we ask the Holy Spirit to break us and fill us daily with His holy love.

Several weeks ago I had the opportunity to lead a church in a period of repentance, cleansing and pleading with the Lord for a breakthrough of love for lost souls. We all got down on our knees and cried out for God to change us and use us as vessels among those in our neighborhoods and cities. A holy hush came over the room. We sensed the Holy Spirit working among us as we humbled ourselves before Him. Since that day God has given me the privilege to lead four other church groups in such prayer sessions. Each time the Lord touched us deeply as we knelt before Him and pleaded with Him to renew our lives and instill in us a greater evangelistic passion.

What is Your Passion?

What is your passion? It may be golf. Your children. Your grandchildren. Your work. Go ahead and enjoy these pursuits.

They're all blessings from the Lord, designed for our enjoyment. But I call you to join me in asking the Lord for the noblest passion of all—to boldly and compassionately share Christ with everyone possible. Get on your knees and beg the Lord to break forth in a mighty baptism of compassion among the body of Christ where you worship.[7]

Would you pray this prayer with me right now?

> O, Father, please help us to hear your heartbeat for the lost. Give us new hearts, that we may have more of a single-minded devotion to Your great commission. May this call to proclaim the gospel not just be a burden but rather a delight to our souls. Please grant us Your joy, Your passion and Your power as we take this glad news to a world without hope...without Jesus. Break our hearts, dear Father, and mold them into hearts fit for Your use in reaching out to others. It's all for Your glory that we pray, O loving Father. In the sweet name of Jesus we pray, Amen.

Notes

1. 2 Peter 3:9b, *The Message*, translated by Eugene H. Peterson (Colorado Springs, CO: NavPress, 1993), 498.

2. Matthew 9:36

3. Bruce Marchiano, *In the Footsteps of Jesus* (Eugene, OR: Harvest House, 1997), 117.

4. Ed Silvoso, *That None Should Perish* (Ventura, CA: Regal, 1994), 92.

5. Ibid., 94.

6. "Evangelism Fellowship Conference," sponsored by Herald of Truth. Ft. Worth, Texas. November 14, 1998.

7. For a sample guide of a group prayer, see Appendix C, "Praying for the Lost and for Evangelistic Fervor—Leader's Guide."

Twelve

A Final Word

*Prayer is the summit meeting in the very throne
room of the universe. There is no higher level.*

Ralph Herring

Prayer changes history. That may seem like a bold statement.
But I firmly believe that when we humbly ask the living
God to change us and others, He'll use us to change history.
One woman from my church has especially been convicted of
the truth of this statement. Her example of bold prayer has
been a great inspiration to me in writing this book.

Birth of a Prayer Ministry

For the last three years, God has used Carolyn Dycus as a
key leader in establishing an organized prayer ministry at the
Highland Church of Christ in Abilene. Her passion to know
Christ more and to experience His power in prayer led to the
development of Highland's prayer ministry. Carolyn became
convicted that we're not New Testament Christians if we don't
have a prayer life. She longed for a spiritual breakthrough in
her church. With a passion for prayer exploding in her heart,

Carolyn sensed God leading her to give birth to this ministry. While speaking at a women's conference on prayer, Carolyn boldly shared her convictions with these words:

> Are we, as God's chosen representatives on this earth, charged with speeding the coming of the day of the Lord? I see this as an urgent request to believers everywhere to pray for revival in our churches, our cities and in the world, so that everyone will have the opportunity to come to repentance...I believe our Lord wants us to be radical. He tells us to be hot or cold, not lukewarm or "I am about to spit you out of my mouth." (Rev. 3:16)[1]

The work of prayer continually grabbed Carolyn's attention. Three years ago she attended a citywide prayer seminar offered at a community center in Abilene. Terry Tekyl, a man with a vision and fervor for prayer, led the non-denominational sessions on prayer. Burning with the conviction that prayer is key to revival in our land, Tekyl travels throughout the country training believers to establish prayer ministries. After attending the one-day prayer seminar, Carolyn knew that God had led her to it. She felt called by the Lord to jump-start a prayer ministry at our church.

One Step at a Time

One of the greatest lessons Carolyn learned from the prayer seminar is that she should take one step at a time. Tekyl emphasized how vital it is to keep it simple when launching a prayer ministry. Those words were a great comfort to Carolyn since all the information she had been learning about prayer ministries overwhelmed her. Carolyn decided to take one bold step to initiate this new ministry. She began searching for a location in the church to set up a prayer room.

Once the church staff helped her locate a vacated room to set apart for prayer, she realized the need to seek her elders' blessings. Arranging a visit with a group of administrative elders who meet weekly, she entered the meeting with trembling knees. To her delight, she witnessed her shepherds quickly blessing the new prayer ministry. They asked the Lord to guide and empower Carolyn in this new work. She left the meeting feeling elated and anointed by God.

As Carolyn's burden for a flourishing prayer ministry grew, she continued bringing up the subject with her prayer partner, Brenda. After spending a year asking the Lord to open doors for this prayer vision to blossom, one day she sensed God telling her, "It's time to invite more partners to join you." Brenda told Carolyn about an upcoming ministry fair at Highland and suggested that Carolyn set up a booth for her prayer dream. Carolyn felt God tugging at her heart again.

She promptly arranged to have a booth set up for the ministry fair. That Sunday a large number of Highland members, mostly women, signed the information sheet. One man said that he wandered around the ministry fair asking the Lord to lead him to a new way to serve Him. When he saw the prayer ministry booth, he knew that God led him there. As Carolyn later looked at the names of those who signed up, she felt God confirming that He was leading the way. Highland's new prayer ministry had gone public. It would eventually expand in exciting ways.

God Uses Ordinary People

In an interview, Carolyn told me, "I am not a bold person. And I'm not an organized person. But God does use ordinary people. He doesn't pick the most talented people to do His work. And so I claim His strength and am willing to do what needs to be done." As Highland's prayer ministry began to take shape, it became clear that the Lord's strength was upon this woman. She persisted in following God's call to lead out in organized prayer.

While Carolyn felt inadequate in administering the details of the new ministry, God raised up men and women to fill in the gaps. She and several others began to meet on Sunday afternoons once a month to plan the work. Several women from the team worked on equipping and decorating the prayer room. Others helped establish a prayer chain, arranging for one group to be called with prayer requests during the day and another at night. Carolyn and her team began asking various members of the congregation to take turns praying in the prayer room during the Sunday assemblies.

Churches United in Prayer

As the months progressed, more prayer warriors were added to the team and a number of ideas for prayer began to flow into the ministry. One woman from another congregation approached Carolyn about a unique plan for praying for the lost. She asked Highland to join two other churches in publishing a prayer evangelism calendar. Each of the three churches was to periodically submit the names of friends, neighbors and family members who did not yet belong to Christ. At the beginning of each month, she sent a calendar to the churches listing on each day of the month the first names of lost people. When one of these people comes to Christ, the good news appears on the next calendar. As Highland's organized prayer ministry grows, more and more members are actively praying for the lost.

Answering God's Call

The Lord may be calling you to begin or expand your church's prayer ministry as He called Carolyn. If you feel frightened or inadequate as Carolyn did when taking baby steps in her adventure of prayer, you're in good company. Moses also felt very inadequate to lead the Israelites. Gideon realized his deep inadequacy in leading an army. Mary knew she was unworthy in giving birth to the Son of God.

Whenever God has called me to a task that I know is beyond my human abilities, He brings to mind the words of a wise friend: "When God calls you, He qualifies you." If you sense the Lord calling you to encourage your church to begin a prayer evangelism ministry, He will qualify you.

Joined with the Eternal Intercessor

We are not alone in this work of intercession. The great Intercessor, Jesus Christ, is in the throne room working on our behalf. Scripture assures us that "Christ Jesus, who died— more than that, who was raised to life—is at the right hand of God and is also interceding for us."[2]

Richard Foster reinforces this truth that our Lord Jesus Christ is the Great Intercessor:

> Our ministry of intercession is made possible only because of Christ's continuing ministry of intercession…Jesus Christ our eternal Intercessor is responsible for our prayer life…his prayers sustain our desires to pray, urging us on and giving us hope of being heard. The sight of Jesus in his heavenly intercession gives us strength to pray in his name.[3]

Isn't it empowering to know that we are not alone as we pray and call others to this work of intercession? One dramatic story from the last century serves as a strong reminder of what God can do when His people unite in intercessory prayer.

Five Days in May

Sixty years ago the free world was embroiled in a terrifying war. For seven years Adolf Hitler led Nazi Germany to crush one country after another. On May 24, 1940, the Western Allies were facing a military and political crisis. From a human standpoint, the situation appeared hopeless.

500,000 French and British troops were trapped in the small coastal town of Dunkirk. Hitler's armed forces were only 15 miles away and appeared on the verge of crushing the allied army. If the British had surrendered at this point, it's likely that the outcome of the war would have been tragic. Hitler's military terror may have continued reigning for many more years. A number of influential leaders were predicting this moment as the end of the British Empire. One king declared that the cause of the allies was lost. Even Winston Churchill's confidence was momentarily shaken. It was a very bleak time in our history. Behind the scenes, however, Almighty God was at work—stirring up a group of Christian believers who were convinced that there was a much greater Ally working on their behalf.

On May 24, several churches in England called for a nationwide day of prayer to be held on Sunday, May 26. Within 24 hours of this declaration, Hitler suddenly ordered his troops to halt. On the evening of the day of prayer, another dramatic event occurred. An order was issued in England to deliver all the troops trapped at Dunkirk. Every water craft available was sent across the English Channel to rescue as many allied troops as possible before the German Army arrived. As thousands of English boats headed for the shores of France, God continued to work miracles during those pivotal five days in May.

For the next three days, Hitler's armies unexplainably stayed in place—only a few miles from Dunkirk. By June 1, 336,000 men were safely delivered from Dunkirk to the shores of England. The leaders of England were overjoyed and stunned. Reflecting upon this dramatic turning point in the war, Winston Churchill offered this sobering observation: "If Germany had defeated either (Britain or France) or both, she would give no mercy; we should be reduced to the status of vassals forever."[4]

It's obvious that God responded to the English people's prayers and caused a momentous turning point in World War II. As I read this story, the application to my life and the present day church became obvious. The war in which we're engaged is of even greater significance.

God's Call for More Prayer Warriors

Millions and millions of lost souls are huddled on the shores of a lost world. Satan is attacking them and threatening to bring them to destruction. They're standing on the brink of eternity, trapped by the devil, "who has taken them captive to do his will."[5]

Our Lord loves these captives and longs to save them from the enemy, "not wanting anyone to perish, but everyone to come to repentance."[6] He's given us disciples the awesome privilege of bringing good news to the captives. And He uses the proclamation of the gospel and our fervent prayers to rescue these precious souls from the "Dunkirk" of sin. He longs to bring them safely to the shores of heaven.

Your church may be standing at a pivotal point in its history. It could be that your congregation is locked in the stalemate of warring factions. Perhaps your leaders are ruled more by fear than by the Holy Spirit. When fear and in-house squabbles

affect a church, it becomes derailed from its mission of bringing souls to Jesus.

Before you read any further, I want you to stop and pray
that the Spirit of the living God will speak to your heart about
becoming a mighty prayer warrior in your church. That He
will use you, as ordinary and unqualified as you might feel, to
implement ideas I mentioned in this book. To use you as the
next Carolyn in your congregation.

This is an exciting challenge, one with a great responsibil-
ity. It's a high calling reserved for believers who are willing to
allow the Holy Spirit to flow through them in a mighty way.
Jesus has promised to work with us. May we call upon His
power and guidance each day, asking Him to deepen our
prayer lives individually and as a church. As we continually get
on our knees, may the living God respond to our prayers by
drawing lost people to His Son and adding them to His church.
I truly believe that as we become more serious about prayer,
the Lord will move in remarkable ways.

For five crucial days in May, believers in Christ throughout
England pleaded with Almighty God to intervene in a war.
God answered their pleas, turning the corner of the war. The
same God wants to bestow His power upon us as we wage a
war on behalf of eternal souls. Let's allow the Lord to work in
us to change history. It all begins when we get on our knees.
Won't you join me?

Dear Father,

I lift before Your throne every brother and sister in Christ
who has read this book. May You give them a mighty vision
for prayer evangelism in their church. As they heed Your call,
please remind them that:

Through Your Presence, they are not alone…

"surely I am with you always, to the very end of the age." — Jesus, Matt. 28:20b

When they lose their focus, they can return continually to the cross…

"May I never boast except in the cross of our Lord Jesus Christ, through which the world has been crucified to me, and I to the world." — Gal. 6:14

When they feel weak and inadequate in this prayer mission, You will infuse them with Your power…

"'Not by might nor by power, but by my Spirit,' says the LORD Almighty." — Zeph. 4:6

"My grace is sufficient for you, for my power is made perfect in weakness." — 2 Cor. 12:9

Use these willing servants of Yours to ignite a revival in their church and their city. May You use their gifts, passion and works of prayer to draw many unsaved people into a relationship with You.

Lord, we want millions more voices to join the chorus of praise to You. Please use our prayers and prayer ministries to expand the chorus, for You are worthy to be praised.

In the awesome and beautiful Name of Jesus, Amen.

Notes

1. Carolyn Dycus, Ladies' Retreat in Edmond, OK, October 2, 1999.

2. Romans 8:34

3. Richard Foster, *Prayer: Finding the Heart's True Home* (San Francisco: Harper Collins, 1992), 193.

4. James Dobson, "Family News from Dr. James Dobson," May 2000. He quoted extensively from the book by John Lukacs, *Five Days in London: May 1940* (New Haven, CT: Yale University Press, 1999).

5. 2 Timothy 2:26

6. 2 Peter 3:9b

Appendix A

Suggestions for Starting a Prayer Room

1. Pray for the guidance of the Holy Spirit in starting this ministry. Recognize that a prayer ministry is significant in empowering all the other ministries of the church. A prayer room is a tangible way of declaring that your church is a house of prayer.

2. Find a room (or rooms) that can be designated for this purpose. In the best case scenario, this room should be accessed easily from the outside and be heated and cooled independently. Think creatively.

3. Purchase a notebook binder and some dividers with labels. Suggested labels to go with the start-up kit categories would be: ADORATION, CONFESSION, THANKSGIVING, SUPPLICATION. Label the notebook, "Prayer Room."

4. Purchase 2 spiral notebooks.

   a. Label one notebook, "Sign-in Log for Prayer Room: Please sign in each time you pray. This serves as encouragement to others and as accountability to you." Create columns in the notebook for date, time prayed, and signature.

   b. Label the other notebook, "The Deeds of God: A Record of Answered Prayer at (name of your church)." Sit down and try to enter a backlog of some obvious answered prayers in your church over the past two or three years. This spiral notebook will be used during the Thanksgiving time.

5. Purchase a card-file box and some note cards. Label the box, "Prayer Request Box." Write down some known prayer requests and enter them on cards. Be sure to include on the cards the day on which the request was entered so that the box can be purged periodically. Sources for obtaining these specific requests can include:

a. Requests that those praying in the Prayer Room write down.

b. Prayer request slips in the pews that are placed in the offering plate.

c. Prayer requests that are called into the church office, given to the prayer coordinator or left on the prayer room telephone recorder.

Create one card that sticks out above the rest that reads, "The last person who prayed stopped here."

6. Personalize some of the supplication sheets in the start-up kit with the following: pictures, addresses, a map of your city or county, a copy of your church's vision and mission statements and your goals for that year (and each year until faith becomes sight).

7. Create some door hangers that say on one side, "PRAYER IN SESSION" and on the other side, "PRAYER ROOM – COME ON IN."

8. Put a hymnal, Bible and any other prayer helps in the Prayer Room.

9. Coordinate with your minister and worship committee a Kick-Off Sunday, where he preaches on prayer and then concludes with an opportunity to sign up for an hour slot in the Prayer Room. Encourage your minister to model prayer by signing up himself.

10. Ask people to sign up for specific hour time slots; i.e. to make a commitment to pray every Thursday from 12 Noon to 1:00 p.m. for 8 weeks or 3 months. At the end of that 8 weeks or 3 months, they can decide whether or not to recommit for another time period.

11. Send "Thank You" notes to those who pray in the Prayer Room.

12. Periodically share in your church newsletter, bulletin or pulpit announcements some of the answers to prayers that are being recorded.

Note: These ideas are adapted from the guidelines of the prayer room of the Highland Church of Christ in Abilene, Texas. Compiled by Carolyn Dycus. The original source for some of this material is Terry Teykl, *Making Room to Pray* (Muncie, IN: Prayer Point Press).

Appendix B

*Suggestions for Prayer Room Procedure During a Worship Assembly**

PROMISES:

One of the rewarding privileges of participating in the Prayer Room Ministry during the morning worship assemblies is that we are reminded that God has provided us with special promises. For example, see Matthew 17:20b-21; Matthew 6:6; Matthew 7:7-8; John 14:12-13. Can any gift be greater? Use these promises as guides to pray for God's Spirit to move in the heart and words of those preaching and leading worship to touch the hearts of God's people through music, praise, and proclamation of God's word. Pray especially for those who have a specific need for guidance this morning. May God bless your time together in this mighty hour of prayer.

PREPARE FOR PRAYER:

1. Purge yourself of uncleanness (Matthew 18:21,22).
2. Ask for forgiveness (Mark 11:24-25).
3. Push evil away and stand up for Christ (Ephesians 6:13-17).
4. Come boldly before the throne of God (Hebrews 4:16).
5. Know that God is hearing you (I Peter 3:12a).
6. Claim the power of earnest praying (James 5:16).
7. Recognize that power is released in prayer (Isaiah 55:11).

8. Plan to pray in the name of Jesus Christ (John 16:23,24).

9. Know that through prayer, God can change the lives of others (Daniel 6:10-27 and Chapter 9).

10. Realize you are to pray always, never giving up (Luke 18:1-7).

ALLOW THE HOLY SPIRIT TO LEAD YOU IN PRAYER (YOU MAY CHOOSE TO FOLLOW THE OUTLINE BELOW).

WORSHIPERS IN MEDITATION:

• Pray that people will recognize the presence of God in this assembly today (Matthew 18:20).

• Realize how helpless we are without the indwelling Intercessor, the Holy Spirit, our Instructor in prayer (Romans 8:26).

WORSHIPERS IN PRAYER

• Pray for those who lead prayers during the assembly.

• Ask the Lord to give them strength and courage in their meditation (Philippians 4:6; Matthew 18:19).

WORSHIPERS THROUGH SONG AND PRAISE

• Ask that the Lord will be pleased with our sacrifice of praise (Hebrews 13:15).

• Ask that we will encourage one another with thanksgiving to God (Colossians 3:16).

• Pray for the congregation to make melody in their hearts to our Lord (Ephesians 5:19), and that we would rejoice in song for His gifts to us (Psalm 105:2).

• Pray for the worship leader and all individuals who are ministering in a special way through music.

WORSHIPERS RECEIVING GOD'S WORD

• Pray for a special spirit of reverence to come now into the assembly (Leviticus 19:30).

• Pray that the Lord will speak through the preacher and through others speaking God's word in the pulpit.

• Pray that the people of the congregation will have receptive hearts (James 4:8).

• Pray for the people to be focused on Christ and not to be distracted (Isaiah 5:27).

• Pray for the Holy Spirit to clarify scripture to everyone and to convict the unsaved (2 Peter 3:9).

• Pray that the sermon will impart knowledge of God's character and His will for us in our daily walk (Jeremiah 3:15).

• Pray for the Holy Spirit to empower each believer with wisdom to know Him better (Ephesians 1:17-19).

WORSHIPERS AT THE LORD'S TABLE

• Pray for discernment for each participant in proclaiming the Lord's death until he comes (1 Corinthians 11:23-3:32).

• Pray for each participant to understand in a personal way that Christ's body was broken and His blood was shed for him or her for the forgiveness of their sins (Matthew 26:26-29).

WORSHIPERS AT BAPTISM

• Pray for God's protection of the new Christian, and that he/she be one with Christ (John 17:20-26).

• Pray for the one being baptized to be filled with joy in understanding he/she is dead to sin and alive in Christ — that he/she is freed from sin's power (Romans 6:3-7).

• Pray for the congregation to identify with freedom from the world's bondage (Romans 6:15-23).

• Pray for the congregation to commit to help this new Christian in whatever way we can (1 Corinthians 12:27-28).

WORSHIPERS THROUGH DEDICATION

- Pray for the lost to be saved (Acts 16:31).
- Pray for rededication of lives to Christ to occur in the service (Hosea 14:4).
- Pray for those who feel led to place their membership with the church (1 Corinthians 3:9).
- Pray for those who feel a special call to commit to serve in the church or in God's harvest fields wherever they may be (2 Thessalonians 1: 11,12).
- Pray for the church to minister to those making decisions (Galatians 6:10).

BENEDICTION

- Pray that the indwelling Spirit will guide our daily activities throughout the week (Psalm 48:14).
- Pray that the Lord will watch over us when we depart from this place (Genesis 31:49).

*These guidelines were compiled by Carolyn Dycus and are partially drawn from the prayer ministry of the First United Methodist Church in Abilene, Texas, and from Terry Teykl, *Making Room to Pray* (Muncie, IN: Prayer Point Press). Contact information: 1 (888) 656-6067 / www.prayerpointpress.com

Appendix C

*Praying for the Lost
and for Evangelistic Fervor*

Leader's Guide

I. Introduction

A. Ed Silvoso tells of the time when he first became a Christian. He was very zealous in sharing Christ with the lost. However, as the years went by he became more theologically educated and began to care less for unsaved people.

1. Then he felt hit by a two-by-four when he re-read 2 Peter 3:9 –"The Lord is not slow in keeping his promise, as some understand slowness. He is patient with you, not wanting anyone to perish, but everyone to come to repentance."

2. Ed said, "I fell on my knees and cried out to God for a baptism of compassion for the lost. As I repented of my spiritual complacency, God's grace washed away the apathy...God's love flooded my soul and restored the joy of my salvation." [From *That None Should Perish* by Ed Silvoso (Ventura, CA: Regal, 1994), 94.]

B. Think about your own story. Has your zeal for the unsaved diminished? In order to encourage your church to become more concerned for those who don't know Christ, the following prayer guide can be used in small group settings, Bible classes or with the entire church.

II. Prayer Time

A. In 1 Cor. 5:4, Paul said – "When you are assembled in the name of our Lord Jesus and I am with you in spirit, and the power of our Lord Jesus is present…"

B. I want to remind you that the Lord Jesus is present here with us. For the next 30 minutes I want to lead you in a prayer time where we'll invite the Lord to transform our hearts so that we'll have a greater compassion for the lost and a more fervent zeal in reaching them with the gospel.

C. I invite you to get on your knees before the living God as we together enter His throne room through the blood of Jesus.

D. Adoration

1. Let's begin our time before the Father by praising Him for Who He is. Listen to God's Word as He proclaims His power and holiness and sovereignty:

a. "You are my witnesses," declares the LORD, "and my servant whom I have chosen, so that you may know and believe me and understand that I am he….I, even I, am the LORD, and apart from me there is no savior. I have revealed and saved and proclaimed… You are my witnesses," declares the LORD, "that I am God." — Isa. 43:10a, 11-12

b. "I, even I, am he who blots out your transgressions, for own sake, and remembers your sins no more." — Isa. 43:25

c. "This is what the LORD says—your Redeemer, the Holy One of Israel: "I am the LORD your God, who teaches you what is best for you, who directs you in the way you should go." — Isa. 48:17

d. "Do not be afraid. I am the First and the Last. I am the Living One; I was dead, and behold I am alive for ever and

ever! And I hold the keys of death and Hades." — Rev.
1:17b-18

e. "Behold, I am coming soon! My reward is with me, and
I will give to everyone according to what he has done. I am
the Alpha and the Omega, the First and the Last, the
Beginning and the End. Blessed are those who wash their
robes, that they may have the right to the tree of life and may
go through the gates into the city." — Rev 22:12-14

2. For a few moments, let's just praise God for Who He is.

3. "Great (are You) LORD and most worthy of praise." —
1 Chron. 16:25

E.   Confession

1. As we encounter the greatness and holiness of God, let's
now confess our sins—both individually and as a church.

2. When Isaiah entered the temple he heard the seraphs cry
out "Holy, Holy, Holy." In the presence of His holiness, Isaiah
felt absolutely naked and shattered because he recognized his
sinfulness.

3. As we come into the presence of the holiness of God, we
recognize that our righteousness is as filthy rags. We may look
good on the outside, but on the inside we still struggle with such
sins as greed, unforgiveness, self-centeredness, jealousy of others, grumbling, bitterness towards elders, anger towards the
institutional church.

4. Let's search our hearts and have a moment of silent confession of our sins.

5. Prayer: Father, we confess our sins. As a church, we have
at times been guilty in our evangelism of lifting up the church
or a plan or a system...rather than lifting up Jesus. Forgive us,
dear Lord. We're guilty of being exclusive and proud and close-

minded. Cleanse us of our sins, dear Lord, as a church and in each of our hearts. Create in us a new heart, a steadfast spirit. O, Jesus, we need You so desperately in our lives — every day, every moment. Forgive us of any self-sufficiency. May our sufficiency be completely in You — in Your Holy Spirit living within us, in Your word and in what You have done for us on the cross and in the resurrection. May we realize that right now You are interceding on our behalf as You are seated at the right hand of the Father.

F. Thanksgiving

1. Listen to the good news of the gospel in Titus 3, what Jesus has done for us—all by His grace:

"At one time we too were foolish, disobedient, deceived and enslaved by all kinds of passions and pleasures. We lived in malice and envy, being hated and hating one another. But when the kindness and love of God our Savior appeared, he saved us, not because of righteous things we had done, but because of his mercy. He saved us through the washing of rebirth and renewal by the Holy Spirit, whom he poured out on us generously through Jesus Christ our Savior, so that, having been justified by his grace, we might become heirs having the hope of eternal life." — Titus 3:3-7

2. Think for a moment where all of us would be without Jesus.

3. Let's now ponder our many blessings in Christ:

I'll name a few and then allow you to spontaneously call out our blessings in Christ:

      a. No condemnation
      b. We'll never be separated from His love
      c. We're sons of God
      d. Blameless in God's sight

(Pause and let others call out the blessings)

4. Now let's thank Him for saving us, for all the many blessings we have in Christ. (Short time of silent prayer)

5. Father, we want to thank You for how good You've been to us, letting us experience the many joys of being Your children.

G. Supplication

1. We now want to focus on sharing these blessings with others.

2. Lord, would you please "Restore to (us) the joy of (our) salvation and grant (us) a willing spirit, to sustain (us)… Then (we) will teach transgressors your ways, and sinners will turn back to you." — Ps. 51:12-13

3. I pray for a baptism of compassion in the heart of every person here today. By our own strength, we cannot love the world as You love the world. We need the power of Your Holy Spirit. Lord, You promised us in Romans 5 that You have "poured out (Your) love into our hearts by the Holy Spirit, whom (You have) given us." May we claim that power today, dear Father.

4. For each one of Your children in this room, including me, I ask that You would help us be devoted "to prayer, being watchful and thankful…that (You) may open a door for our message, so that we may proclaim the mystery of Christ…and proclaim it clearly. Lord, please give us wisdom in how we act toward outsiders; (making) the most of every opportunity."
Make our "conversation… full of grace, seasoned with salt, so that (we) may know how to answer everyone." — Col. 4:3-6

5. I ask You, dear Father, that "whenever (we) open (our) mouths, words may be given (us) so that (we) will fearlessly make known the mystery of the gospel…And may we declare Your gospel "fearlessly." — Eph. 6:19

6. Now, Lord, I pray that Your Holy Spirit would bring to our minds the names and faces of lost friends and family members in our lives. (PAUSE) As these people come to mind, we bring them before You, Lord.

7. We also want You to bring to mind our cities. All those who are lost in the communities where we live and serve. The children. The overlooked minorities. The poor that are so often ignored. The divorced and single parents that feel looked down upon by church people. Those with AIDS. Men and women in jail. Who are You calling us to reach in our cities, Lord? We can't reach everyone. Yet there are some who can be reached through our influence—if we're willing to take the gospel to them.

May we hear Your heartbeat for the lost, dear Lord. For You're "not wanting anyone to perish, but everyone to come to repentance." Break our hearts, Lord Jesus. Use us as mighty leaders in our churches, like prophets who stand in the gap between those who are saved and those who are lost.

H. Prayer in groups

1. I'd like us to close our prayer time by standing and getting in groups of three to four. We'll pray together in these groups.

2. We'll take turns sharing from our hearts as each of us prays. I want us to focus on three things while in these groups:

a. Asking the Lord to change our hearts and give us more love for the lost.

b. Praying for lost people we know—praying for them by name.

c. Praying for our cities.

I. Close the prayer time with the whole group singing a praise song.

Recommended for Further Reading

Jim Cymbala, *Fresh Wind, Fresh Fire* (Grand Rapids, MI: Zondervan, 1997)

A soul-stirring description of a church leader who learned to lead his flock on his knees and how God created a congregation that takes seriously the gospel and the power of the Holy Spirit. Cymbala's book has ignited a renewal of prayer in hundreds of churches and thousands of Christians' lives. It has had a profound impact on my prayer life. I recommend it to everyone who is serious about experiencing God's power in his or her life. See also his later books, *Fresh Faith* and *Fresh Power.*

Bill Hybels, *Too Busy Not to Pray* (Downers Grove, IL: InterVarsity, 1988)

One of the most inspiring books I've ever read on prayer. Citing many examples from answered prayer in his life, Hybels provides a biblical foundation for the Christian in how God is both able and willing to become an active part of a believer's life.

Ed Silvoso, *That None Should Perish* (Ventura, CA: Regal, 1994)

Through his story and the story of many other church leaders, Silvoso provides a solid plan for reaching entire cities for Jesus through strategic prayer. He tells an amazing story of how churches in a large city in Argentina united together in prayer. His plan, based on principles from Acts, is adaptable to any community. This is a challenging, mind-stretching and vital resource for the modern church.

C. Peter Wagner, *Churches That Pray* (Ventura, CA: Regal, 1993)

Wagner's book was one of the most significant influences in giving me a vision for prayer evangelism. As a former professor of church growth at Fuller Seminary and an outstanding researcher, Wagner has an immense grasp of how churches throughout the world are evangelizing their communities through organized prayer efforts.